Reading Comprehension
Skills and Strategies
Level 6

Saddleback Publishing, Inc.
Three Watson
Irvine, CA 92618-2767
Web site: www.sdlback.com

Development and Production:
The EDGe

ISBN 1-56254-033-5

Printed in the United States of America

09 08 07 06 05   9 8 7 6 5 4 3 2 1

Table of Contents
Skills

About this Series

This unique series is specially created for you by Saddleback Publishing, Inc., as an exciting supplement to reinforce and extend your classroom reading curriculum. *Reading Comprehension Skills and Strategies* can easily be integrated into basic reading curricula as additional reading lessons: as stand-alone strategy and skill instructional lessons; as across-the-curriculum lessons; or as activities for students with special projects, interests, or abilities.

This series is based on the most current research and thought concerning the teaching of reading comprehension. This series not only sharpens traditional reading comprehension skills (main idea, story plot, topic sentence, sequencing, etc.), but it also reinforces the critical reading comprehension strategies that encourage your students to use prior knowledge, experiences, careful thought, and evaluation to help them decide how to practically apply what they know to all reading situations.

Traditional comprehension skills recently have been woven into the larger context of strategy instruction. Today, literacy instruction emphasizes learning strategies—those approaches that coordinate the various reading and writing skills and prior knowledge to make sense to the learner. Our goal in this series is to provide you and your students with the most up-to-date reading comprehension support, while teaching basic skills that can be tested and evaluated.

Reading Comprehension Strategies

- vocabulary knowledge
- activating prior knowledge
- pre-reading—previewing and predicting
- previewing and predicting text
- mental imaging
- self-questioning
- summarizing
- semantic mapping

Saddleback Publishing, Inc., promotes the development of the whole child with particular emphasis on combining solid skill instruction with creativity and imagination. This series gives your students a variety of opportunities to apply reading comprehension strategies as they read, while reinforcing basic reading comprehension skills. In addition, we designed this series to help you make an easy transition between levels (grades 5, 6, and 7) in order to reinforce or enhance needed skill development for individual students.

About this Book

Reading Comprehension Skills and Strategies is designed to reinforce and extend the reading skills of your students. The fun, high-interest fiction and non-fiction selections will spark the interest of even your most reluctant reader. The book offers your students a variety of reading opportunities—reading for pleasure, reading to gather information, and reading to perform a task. Characters throughout the book prompt the student to apply one of the strategies to the reading selection and includes a relevant comprehension skill activity.

Choosing Instructional Approaches

You can use the pages in this book for independent reinforcement or extension, whole group lessons, pairs, or small cooperative groups rotating through an established reading learning center. You may choose to place the activities in a center and reproduce the answer key for self-checking. To ensure the utmost flexibility, the process for managing this is left entirely up to you because you know what works best in your classroom.

Assessment

Assessment and evaluation of student understanding and ability is an ongoing process. A variety of methods and strategies should be used to ensure that the student is being assessed and evaluated in a fair and comprehensive manner. Always keep in mind that the assessment should take into consideration the opportunities the student had to learn the information and practice the skills presented. The strategies for assessment are left for you to determine and are dependent on your students and your particular instructional plan. You will find a Scope & Sequence chart at the back of this book to assist you as you develop your assessment plan.

What do plants have to do with reading? Roots! In both plants and reading, everything grows from roots. Learn these roots and watch your vocabulary grow.

Directions: *Match each word on a leaf to the root from which it grew. Write the letter of the root on the leaf.*

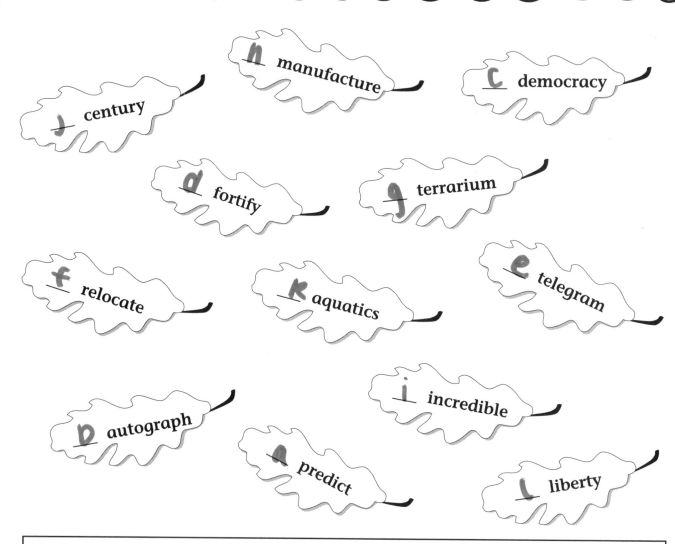

_J_ century

_h_ manufacture

_c_ democracy

_d_ fortify

_g_ terrarium

_f_ relocate

_k_ aquatics

_e_ telegram

_b_ autograph

_a_ predict

_i_ incredible

_l_ liberty

ROOT WORDS

A. dict–say; speak
B. auto–self
C. dem–people; population
D. fort–strong

E. gram–draw; write
F. loc–place
G. terra–earth; land
H. man–hand

I. cred–believe
J. cent–hundred
K. aqua–water
L. liber–to free

Name: Patsy Surdam

Date: _____

Directions: *Read each list of words. Think about how they are alike. Then circle the correct meaning of their common root word.*

1. transport, import, export, portable

   The root "port" most likely means   a. carry   b. ship   c. across

2. diameter, metric, speedometer, centimeter

   The root "meter" most likely means   a. distance   b. machine   c. measure

3. audience, audition, audible, auditory

   The root "aud" most likely means   a. speed   b. hear   c. people

4. construction, instruct, destruct, structure

   The root "struct" most likely means   a. build   b. destroy   c. stop

5. circus, circle, circular, circumstances

   The root "circ" most likely means   a. fun   b. around   c. five

6. proceed, exceed, succeed, concede

   The root "cede or ceed" most likely means   a. go, yield   b. fail   c. obvious

7. signature, signal, sign, significant

   The root "sign" most likely means   a. name   b. mark   c. visible

8. minor, minute, miniature, minimum

   The root "min" most likely means   a. most   b. less   c. small

9. thermos, thermometer, thermal, thermostat

   The root "therm" most likely means   a. bacteria   b. enclosed   c. heat

10. solitary, solo, solely, solitude

    The root "sol" most likely means   a. alone   b. free   c. near

11. unicorn, uniform, unit, united

    The root "uni" most likely means   a. one   b. kind   c. form

Name: Patsy Surdam   **Date:** _____

How do you grow new words? One way is to start with a sprout of a root word, then add a prefix.

Directions: Add the prefix given to the root word. Then, in the sentences below, fill in the correct word from the ones you wrote.

Prefix	Root Word	New Word
dis–opposite of	appear	_____
re–again	write	_____
mis–wrongly	understood	_____
multi–many	color	_____
mid–middle	day	_____
non–not	sense	_____
un–not	necessary	_____
inter–between	national	_____

1. The beautiful butterfly had _____ wings.

2. Sometimes I wish this mess in my room would just _____.

3. On a warm day it is _____ to bring a heavy coat.

4. He was mad because he _____ what I said.

5. The teacher made me _____ my essay.

6. By _____ the sun was high and we were hungry.

7. Olympic athletes enjoy _____ fame.

8. Dad thought my excuse was pure _____.

Name: _____   **Date:** _____

The Bear Facts

The word "bear" can conjure up a variety of images—from a sweet teddy to the untamed force of a grizzly. There are actually seven species of bear and many subspecies. Their size, appearance, habitat, and diet differ greatly. The polar bear and grizzly are the indisputable kings of the bears.

The largest of the bears is the polar bear. It roams the harsh arctic, undaunted by the cold. The key to its survival there lies in its coat. Over a dense underfur lie long hairs that get matted when wet and help keep the skin dry. Seals are its main prey, and ice floes provide a base of operations on its incessant quest for food.

The grizzly has immense physical strength and mobility. Once these bears roamed much of North America, but due to human intrusion, they have retreated to mainly northern remote areas. Though easily capable of knocking down a bison, this bear prefers to indulge in berries and roots. And yes, this brown bear does steal honey from bees' nests.

Despite their differences, these two kinds of bears are so closely related that the two can interbreed and produce fertile hybrid offspring.

1. fur that lies below:_____

2. not able to argue with: _____

3. never ceasing: _____

4. withdrew; moved back: _____

5. invasion: _____

6. variety listed under a species: _____

7. not hampered or discouraged: _____

8. mate between species: _____

9. wild: _____

Got a root word? Then you can grow new words from it by adding suffixes.

Directions: *The missing word in each passage below is an adverb ending in -ly. Find the one that makes the most sense, and fill it in.*

| confidently | nervously | jubilantly | wearily |
| suspiciously | contentedly | dejectedly |

1. The math teacher challenged the class with a particularly tricky problem. "Any volunteers?" he asked with a wry smile. One hand went up. "I'll try it," Linda said

   _____.

2. The Bobcats were favored to win the championship. They were playing well but in the last few seconds, missed a goal and lost. The players hung their heads and left the field

   _____.

3. Mom volunteered to make Kyle's Halloween costume. It took longer than she anticipated. At 11:30 P.M., she was still working, sewing on the last bit of trim. "Just a few more stitches and I'll finally be done, " she said _____.

4. In his whole life Brian had never won anything. When he heard about the science fair, he was determined to make the best project. For weeks he worked on it until it was perfect. When the judges made their decision, Brian _____ accepted the first place ribbon.

5. The doctor told Tim that he had an infection but that an antibiotic should clear it right up. "Do I have to have a shot?" he asked

   _____.

6. Sam left his sandwich on the porch steps and went inside to get a glass of milk. When he came back out, the sandwich was gone. Sam looked over at his dog, Renny,

   _____.

Reading Comprehension • Saddleback Publishing, Inc. ©2002   10   3 Watson, Irvine, CA 92618•Phone (888)SDL-BACK•www.sdlback.com

Word Box

lotion
mention
promotion
nation
description
commotion
accumulation
situation
translation
invention
punctuation
station
prevention
formation
determination
population

1. It snowed all night, so there was an

_____

of several inches by morning.

2. I cannot read Spanish. I'll need a

_____.

3. Oscar did a good job, so he got a raise

and a _____.

4. The geese flew overhead in a V-shaped

_____.

5. The party for Josh is a secret, so don't

_____ it.

6. Vaccinations are given for the

_____ of disease.

7. At midnight, the train pulled into the

_____.

8. The police were looking for a car with

that _____.

9. Due to loss of habitat, the manatee

_____ is decreasing.

10. Every sentence should end with the

correct _____.

Reading Comprehension • Saddleback Publishing, Inc. ©2002   11   3 Watson, Irvine, CA 92618•Phone (888)SDL-BACK•www.sdlback.com

Directions: *Origami is the art of paper folding. It can be complicated or simple. Below are the steps for making a simple folded animal face, but they are out of order! First, using the illustrations as clues, write the steps in the correct order. Then follow the directions to make your own fold-a-face.*

Fold-a-Face

- Fold (A) down so that the point extends below the base of the triangle.
- Begin with a sheet of rectangular paper. Make it square by folding it diagonally, then cutting off the excess strip.
- Color and use cut paper or other materials to create the face of a cat, leopard, or tiger, dog or even a bat.
- Once you have cut off the strip, you will have a large triangle shape. Hold the triangle with the widest angle (A) up.
- Fold up corners (B) and (C) along the edges of flap (A) to form ears.

1. _____
_____
_____

2. _____
_____
_____

3. _____
_____
_____

4. _____
_____
_____

5. _____
_____
_____

Name: _____   **Date:** _____

Part 1: *Match each word to its meaning.*

enormous	a. not fit to eat
inedible	b. easy to reach or get to
accessible	c. able to read and write
spatter	d. sparkle; glitter; shine
diminish	e. thoughtful in a serious manner
glisten	f. to make or become smaller
literate	g. very large; huge
pensive	h. scatter or fall in drops

Part 2: *Complete the puzzle by filling in the words above in alphabetical order.*

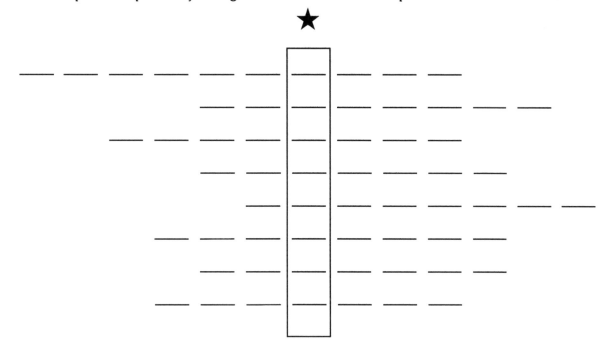

Part 3: *Write the word formed by the letters under the ★. Make sure it matches the meaning given, then write the word in the blank of the sentence.*

__ __ __ __ __ __ __ __ : likely to occur soon; about to happen

The clouds darkened and rain was _____.

Name: _____   Date: _____

How can closing your eyes help you read better? By letting you form a picture in your mind. Then you can go back and see if the words match your ideas.

Directions: *Read the story, then fill in the bubble of the correct answer.*

In the course of evolution, what happens when an area is cut off from the rest of the world? Madagascar is an island 250 miles off the coast of Africa. It is estimated that it has been cut off from the mainland for perhaps 80 million years. The island today is a refuge for many forms of life that have become rare or extinct in other parts of the world. For example, up to 80 percent of Madagascar's plant species are unique to the island. In addition, about 46 kinds of birds are found nowhere else. Lemurs, which elsewhere were unable to compete with their larger primate cousins, the monkeys, continue to thrive in the isolation of Madagascar.

1. Which word refers to *a change over time*?
   O estimation   O evolution   O isolation

2. Madagascar is an island off the _____ coast of Africa.
   O east   O west   O south

3. Lemurs are _____.
   O mammals   O birds   O plants

4. Which best describes the meaning of *unique*?
   O special   O alone   O one of a kind

5. Which word means *a safe place*?
   O rare   O thrive   O refuge

6. What percentage of Madagascar's plants are not unique to the island?
   O 80%   O 20%   O 46%

7. Madagascar is isolated because _____.
   O it is an island   O it is part of Africa   O no one goes there

AFRICA

Name: _____   **Date:** _____

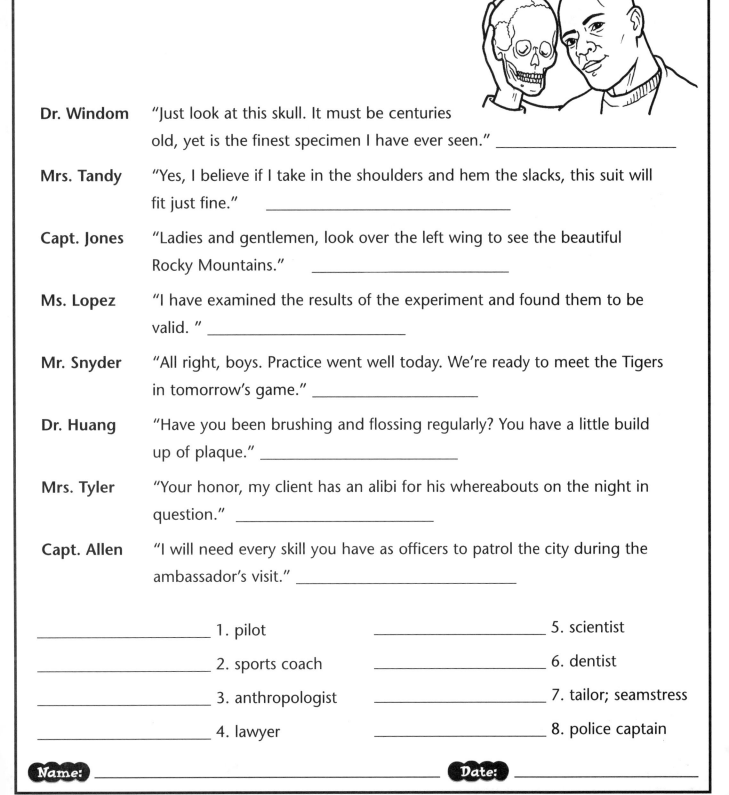

Dr. Windom   "Just look at this skull. It must be centuries old, yet is the finest specimen I have ever seen." _____

Mrs. Tandy   "Yes, I believe if I take in the shoulders and hem the slacks, this suit will fit just fine." _____

Capt. Jones   "Ladies and gentlemen, look over the left wing to see the beautiful Rocky Mountains." _____

Ms. Lopez   "I have examined the results of the experiment and found them to be valid. " _____

Mr. Snyder   "All right, boys. Practice went well today. We're ready to meet the Tigers in tomorrow's game." _____

Dr. Huang   "Have you been brushing and flossing regularly? You have a little build up of plaque." _____

Mrs. Tyler   "Your honor, my client has an alibi for his whereabouts on the night in question." _____

Capt. Allen   "I will need every skill you have as officers to patrol the city during the ambassador's visit." _____

_____ 1. pilot   _____ 5. scientist

_____ 2. sports coach   _____ 6. dentist

_____ 3. anthropologist   _____ 7. tailor; seamstress

_____ 4. lawyer   _____ 8. police captain

Name: _____   **Date:** _____

Running Late

We were already running late for Sunday services. If we hit all the lights right, we could still make it on time. We made it through the intersection of Clover and Reston without a hitch, then through the light at Greenwood, too. It was looking good. But then we heard the whistle and up ahead saw the big white arms come down across the road.

Dad sighed, "I hope it's not a long one."

Sitting only five cars back, we watched as the engine passed, then 72 freight cars. Finally, the caboose rolled by.

11:10. Quietly we opened the door so as not to disturb the people in the pews. But, to our surprise, the service had not yet started. Five more minutes passed. Then the minister walked to the podium, cleared his throat and said, "We are beginning a bit late this morning. Seems there was quite a long train that held up some folks, and if they can wait, so can we."

1. The family was going to church.

_____

2. They were delayed by a traffic light not working properly.

_____

3. There were four people in the car.

_____

4. Clover and Reston are streets.

_____

5. The railroad tracks crossed Clover.

_____

6. The train was carrying cargo, not passengers.

_____

7. The writer counted the freight cars as they went by.

_____

8. The word "hitch" in the first paragraph refers to the couplings used to connect railroad cars.

_____

9. The word "we" in the final sentence refers to the minister and the people waiting in the church.

_____

Name: _____ Date: _____

Hey, sometimes ideas are not directly stated. It's up to you to use clues supplied to figure out, or infer, information.

Directions: *Chris mapped out the Connor family tree. Use it to answer the questions below.*

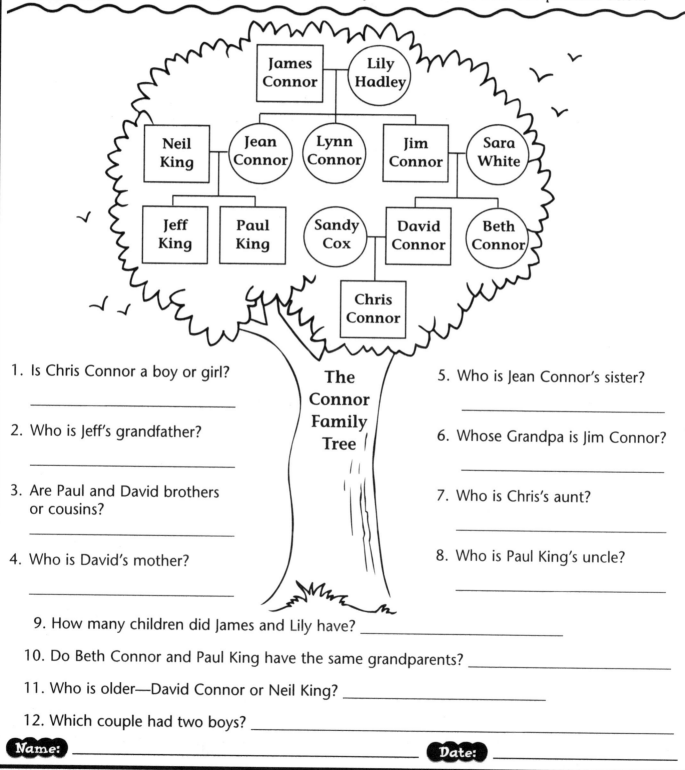

The Connor Family Tree

1. Is Chris Connor a boy or girl?

   _____

2. Who is Jeff's grandfather?

   _____

3. Are Paul and David brothers or cousins?

   _____

4. Who is David's mother?

   _____

5. Who is Jean Connor's sister?

   _____

6. Whose Grandpa is Jim Connor?

   _____

7. Who is Chris's aunt?

   _____

8. Who is Paul King's uncle?

   _____

9. How many children did James and Lily have? _____

10. Do Beth Connor and Paul King have the same grandparents? _____

11. Who is older—David Connor or Neil King? _____

12. Which couple had two boys? _____

Name: _____ **Date:** _____

1. He held the wheel steady and applied the brakes until the **rig** came to a stop.
   - O bike
   - O horse
   - O truck

2. When asked to take her seat, the **impudent** child refused.
   - O young
   - O disrespectful
   - O good-natured

3. Tempers flared and an argument **ensued**.
   - O followed
   - O stopped
   - O south

4. The Chem-Free store caters to people who want **organic** foods.
   - O all-natural
   - O musical
   - O of the body

5. Crows are content to live in the city as well as in **agricultural** regions.
   - O park
   - O farm; rural
   - O unpopulated

6. The king **accumulated** riches while ignoring the needs of the poor.
   - O counted
   - O gave away
   - O collected

7. The couple married under a **canopy** of silk and flowers.
   - O overhead covering
   - O a carpet
   - O painting

8. Before deciding to move, the family had a **frank** discussion about it.
   - O quiet; solemn
   - O a person
   - O honest; open

9. The red blotches **manifested** on his skin indicated an allergic reaction.
   - O visible
   - O celebrated
   - O directly

10. We enjoyed hearing the **saga** of Humphrey the Humpback Whale.
    - O tale; story
    - O sadness
    - O sounds

Name: _____   **Date:** _____

If you come to an unfamiliar word, use the words around it for clues to its meaning. If that doesn't help, get out the trusty dictionary!

Directions: *Write the word that best describes how you would feel in each situation.*

How Would You Feel?

1. The honor roll was just posted on the board. When you check for your name, there it is.

   You feel _____.

   elated   amused

2. You hoped your favorite team would make it to the finals, but they were eliminated.

   You feel _____.

   disappointed   determined

3. During class you look down and notice you're wearing two different colored socks.

   You feel _____.

   flattered   foolish

4. Someone accused you of stealing some money from his backpack.

   You feel _____.

   insulted   inspired

5. You forgot to water Mom's favorite plant as she asked, and it died.

   You feel _____.

   rejected   remorseful

Name: _____ **Date:** _____

1. The two old women sat **reminiscing** about their girlhood.

   Is reminiscing *remembering, crying,* or *complaining?* _____

2. Large rocks **protruded** from the side of the mountain.

   Were the rocks *falling, sticking out,* or *rising up?* _____

3. They hoped to find suitable **quarters** for the night, but none were available.

   Are quarters *money, fourths,* or *shelter?* _____

4. The field was meant for **grazing**.

   Would it be used for *raising crops, feeding livestock,* or *building on?*

   _____

5. The tribe's storyteller was **legendary**.

   Was the storyteller *an exaggerator, well-known,* or *old?* _____

6. At daybreak each morning, the sailors would **hoist** the flag.

   Did they *put it away, fold it,* or *pull it up?* _____

7. The City Council came up with a **feasible** plan for relieving the traffic congestion.

   Was their plan *unrealistic, reasonable,* or *complicated?* _____

8. The ring was inexpensive because it contained **faux** gems.

   Were the gems *fake, flawed,* or *small?* _____

9. A **multitude** of migrating butterflies rested in the trees.

   Is multitude *a large number, a guarded place,* or *reasonable?* _____

10. The explorers were **plagued** by flies.

    Is plagued *consumed, troubled and annoyed,* or *divided into sections.*

    _____

Name: _____   Date: _____

ACROSS

3. What might leaking water do?
4. Where are pupils and irises found?
6. What might a police officer wear?
8. How might a mouse move?
9. Where might a judge be found?
10. What might be raised on a farm?

DOWN

1. What's found in the middle?
2. What's found on a guitar?
3. Where would a mummy be buried?
5. The sound a parrot might make.
7. Where would a hangar be found?

Word Box

tomb / comb
trickle / tickle
fret / flat
center / circle
court / coarse
hamper / scamper
cattle / cuddle
ears / eyes
badge / budge
airport / airplane
squeak / squawk

Name: _____   Date: _____

Get the signal! Signal words give you, a reader, clues about what is coming or what the author wants to point out—a very useful thing to know.

Directions: On the signs below are several signal words. Figure out which one is missing from each sentence. Write it on the line.

Part 1:
toward
probably
such as
however
immediately

1. I like raw carrots, _____, I don't like them cooked.

2. Go one mile, then _____ make a left turn.

3. This is _____ not a good time to ask you this.

4. The wagon train moved west, _____ the mountains.

5. Use a light color, _____ yellow.

1. The horses pulled up _____ the train.

2. He fouled, _____ losing the game.

3. Young kids should _____ be supervised.

4. She sang well _____ her nervousness.

5. The fireworks were canceled _____ rain.

Part 2:
in spite of
always
due to
alongside
consequently

Name: _____

Date: _____

1. There's **another** reason why many people seem...

   O signals that more is to come   O tells when something is happening

2. **In contrast** to being an only child...

   O signals a conclusion   O signals a comparison is coming

3. And so, **in summary**...

   O shows sequence   O signals a conclusion

4. **In addition** to his other inventions...

   O signals an example will follow   O signals that more is to come

5. **First of all,** gather the materials...

   O shows sequence   O shows where something is happening

6. **To illustrate** this idea...

   O will give a reason for   O signals an example will follow

7. But, Maria felt quite the **opposite** about...

   O signals a change of direction   O signals a conclusion

8. The **primary concern** of the council...

   O signals an important point   O shows uncertainty

9. As a **result** of the report ...

   O signals a comparison   O signals a conclusior

10. The **principle** item to keep in mind ...

    O signals change in direction   O signals importance

11. Scientist think that **perhaps** dinosaurs were...

    O shows uncertainty   O shows sequence

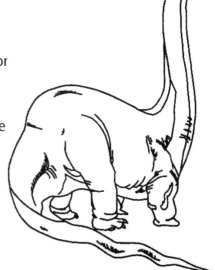

What's a good reader's best friend? The dictionary! It can help you out of plenty of jams, so it's a good idea to get to know it well.

Directions: *Below are ten different meanings for the word field. Decide which meaning applies best in each sentence and write the number.*

field /n/ 1) an open area of land free of woods and buildings
2) an area set aside or used for a sport
3) the location of a military operation
4) land containing a specific natural resource or crop
5) an area or division of study or subject
6) a location for practical use outside a laboratory or organization
7) the visible area
8) the background of a flag
/v/ 9) to handle a ball while playing
10) to answer

_____ A   The bones were found in a coal field.

_____ B   The speaker will field questions from the audience.

_____ C   That tree is blocking my field of vision.

_____ D   Geology was her field of expertise.

_____ E   The flag of Japan is a red circle on a white field.

_____ F   Count on Ty to field the ball.

_____ G   The rabbit family lived in the field.

_____ H   The FBI set up a field observation.

_____ I   Goalposts were set at both ends of the field.

_____ J   For ships, the ocean can be the field of battle.

_____ K   Mr. Jones is responsible for all sales in the field.

_____ L   What field of science do you find most interesting?

_____ M   The computer field is growing fast.

_____ N   Fields of grain stretched for miles.

Name: _____   **Date:** _____

Directions: *Some well-known rhymes and stories meant for "little kids" contain words or phrases they might not understand. Imagine that you have to explain them. Answer the questions below. A dictionary may be helpful.*

1. When the Queen of Hearts baked some **tarts**, what was she making?

   muffins, fruit pies, or *baked apples* _____

2. Little Miss Muffet was eating **curds and whey**. What food is this most similar to?

   cottage cheese, cereal, or *rice pudding* _____

3. When the owl and the pussycat wrapped honey in a **five-pound note**, what was it wrapped in?

   a letter, music box, or *money* _____

4. Mary's little lamb had **fleece** as white as snow. What is fleece?

   feet, face, or *wool* _____

5. When Jack fell down and broke his **crown**, what part of his body was injured?

   tooth, head, or *leg* _____

6. In "Three Billy Goats Gruff," the troll had eyes like saucers and a nose like a **poker**. What is a poker?

   pig, old man, or *metal rod* _____

7. The rat ate the malt that lay in the house that Jack built. What is **malt**?

   a grain, chocolate, or *a spice* _____

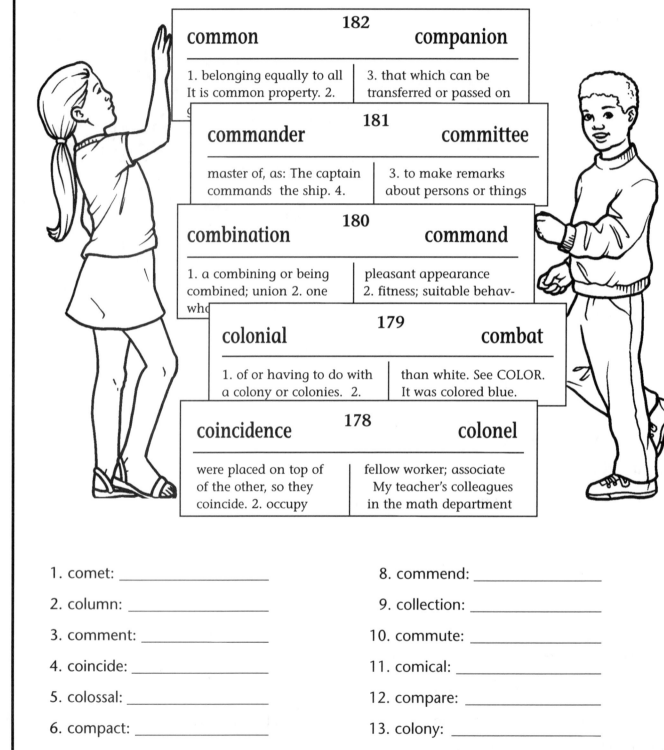

182

common   companion

1. belonging equally to all
It is common property. 2.

3. that which can be
transferred or passed on

181

commander   committee

master of, as: The captain
commands the ship. 4.

3. to make remarks
about persons or things

180

combination   command

1. a combining or being
combined; union 2. one
who

pleasant appearance
2. fitness; suitable behav-

179

colonial   combat

1. of or having to do with
a colony or colonies. 2.

than white. See COLOR.
It was colored blue.

178

coincidence   colonel

were placed on top of
of the other, so they
coincide. 2. occupy

fellow worker; associate
My teacher's colleagues
in the math department

1. comet: _____

2. column: _____

3. comment: _____

4. coincide: _____

5. colossal: _____

6. compact: _____

7. comfort: _____

8. commend: _____

9. collection: _____

10. commute: _____

11. comical: _____

12. compare: _____

13. colony: _____

14. collapse: _____

Name: _____

Date: _____

Tribal Masks

In looking at the variety of African tribal masks, it is easy to appreciate them as an art form. But, unlike other art forms that are created for _____ alone, the tribal masks of Africa often serve a purpose as well. They are used as symbols of status and for specific functions in ceremonies and rituals. Often spiritual beliefs are attached to a particular mask. The wearer of a mask may not only be displaying _____, but may be believing he is protecting himself from unwanted forces as well. A certain mask may be worn during a ritual to protect the group from danger, honor the dead, or celebrate good fortune. Masks are used in entertainment as well—the_____ points in many theatrical skits and dances.

Tribal masks possess a _____of symbolic meanings in a tribe's physical and spiritual lives. In addition to their artistic beauty, they are an _____ part of many tribal cultures.

myriad: _____

focal: _____

aesthetics: _____

integral: _____

prestige: _____

Name: _____ Date: _____

It is amazing how words give you hints and clues while you are reading. Using the words and what you already know helps you unlock the meaning of what you read.

Directions: Read the statements below. Circle the word or words that give you a clue about the answer. Put an X in front of the correct answer.

1. Dana got a package in the mail. It was a ...

___ new car   ___ present from Grandma   ___ pepperoni pizza

2. Jerry picked up the phone and said, "Hello." It was...

___ the mayor   ___ his Uncle Jack   ___ his parrot, Petey

3. Mom carried the heavy load up the stairs. It was filled with...

___ stuffed animals   ___ rocks and dirt   ___ laundry

4. Paul boiled them, then drained them in a colander. He was cooking...

___ meatballs   ___ noodles   ___ cupcakes

5. Tony put a carrot into the cage for Lester. Lester is...

___ his pet snake   ___ his pet rabbit   ___ his best friend

6. Mr. Michaels paid $225 for his purchase. He bought...

___ a new car   ___ a suit   ___ a pair of shoes

7. Allison got her friend Keri a birthday present. It was...

___ a photo album   ___ a computer   ___ an ice cream store

8. Justin opened the front door and greeted both sets of grandparents. There were...

___ four grandparents   ___ six grandparents   ___ two grandparents

Name: _____   **Date:** _____

Read the passage all the way through without stopping. Then on the lines at the bottom of the page write the missing words. Last, write the word or words in the passage that provided clues about each missing word.

Opossums are marsupials, or animals that carry their young in a front __1.__ . They are the only marsupial native to North America.

Adult opossums range in size from as small as a mouse to as large as a house cat. They are strange-looking creatures. They have furry bodies, sharp __2.__ , a pointed __3.__ , and a long, practically hairless __4.__ . Some opossums hang upside-down by their tails.

A mother opossum gives birth to her babies in groups of 5–20. Newborn opossums are very small—about the size of a kidney __5.__ . About 15 infants could fit in a teaspoon! The babies are carried in the mother's pouch for about two months. They stay with the mother for several more weeks as they continue to grow. During this time, she carries them up top on her __6.__ .

When in danger, opossums (also called __7.__) lie still to appear to be dead. This is where the expression "playing __8.__ " comes from.

Missing Word   Clue Word or Words

1. _____   _____

2. _____   _____

3. _____   _____

4. _____   _____

5. _____   _____

6. _____   _____

7. _____   _____

8. _____   _____

Name: _____   **Date:** _____

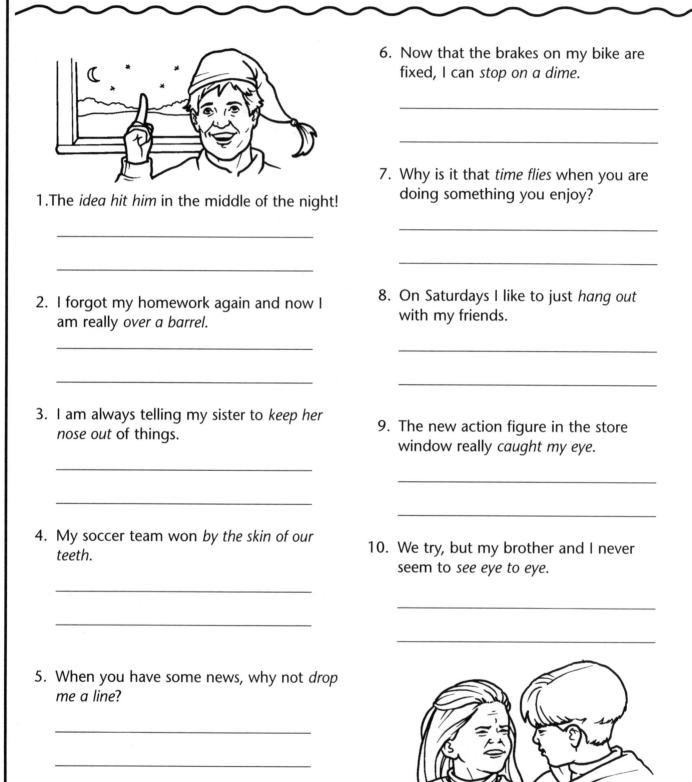

1. The *idea hit him* in the middle of the night!

_____

_____

2. I forgot my homework again and now I am really *over a barrel.*

_____

_____

3. I am always telling my sister to *keep her nose out* of things.

_____

_____

4. My soccer team won *by the skin of our teeth.*

_____

_____

5. When you have some news, why not *drop me a line?*

_____

_____

6. Now that the brakes on my bike are fixed, I can *stop on a dime.*

_____

_____

7. Why is it that *time flies* when you are doing something you enjoy?

_____

_____

8. On Saturdays I like to just *hang out* with my friends.

_____

_____

9. The new action figure in the store window really *caught my eye.*

_____

_____

10. We try, but my brother and I never seem to *see eye to eye.*

_____

_____

You have probably noticed that many stories you read use descriptions that compare something to something else. A comparison using like or as is called a simile—her hair was like silk. A direct comparison—he was a fish out of water—is called a metaphor. Read each statement. Is it a simile, metaphor, or neither?

Comparisons Paint Colorful Descriptions

1. Dad said he'd be late because he still had a mountain of paperwork to do.
   - O simile
   - O metaphor
   - O neither

2. The used car turned out to be a lemon.
   - O simile
   - O metaphor
   - O neither

3. We heard the fire engine coming from blocks away.
   - O simile
   - O metaphor
   - O neither

4. The baby has cheeks like roses and a smile like sunshine.
   - O simile
   - O metaphor
   - O neither

5. What could be in this box—it is as light as a feather!
   - O simile
   - O metaphor
   - O neither

6. The wrestler's arms were as big as tree branches.
   - O simile
   - O metaphor
   - O neither

7. It looked as if we had been walking in circles.
   - O simile
   - O metaphor
   - O neither

8. Don't mind Beth—she eats like a bird.
   - O simile
   - O metaphor
   - O neither

9. The day was growing old and there was still no word from him.
   - O simile
   - O metaphor
   - O neither

Bonus! *Read the title of this page again. Is it a simile or metaphor? Why?* _____

_____

Name: _____ **Date:** _____

Butterflies start their lives as caterpillars. Once they emerge from their cocoons, they display brilliantly colored wings composed of thousands of tiny scales. As caterpillars, they primarily feed on leaves. As butterflies, they live only on liquid nectar from flowering plants. When not in flight, butterflies rest their wings upright. Their antennae are often smooth and club-shaped.

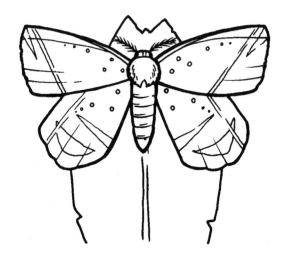

Moths also start their lives as caterpillars, but unlike butterflies, when they emerge from their cocoons their wings are often drab. Yet, their wings often display unique designs and patterns that help them blend into their environment. For example, carpenter moths have wings that look like tree bark. Moths generally hold their wings flat when at rest and many also have feathered antennae.

1. **Who**, when not in flight, rest their wings upright?

    O moths   O butterflies

2. **What** do carpenter moth wings resemble?

    O tree bark   O green leaves

3. **Why** are many moths' wings drab?

    O so they can fly at night   O to blend into their environment

4. **When** do moths hold their wings flat?

    O when they are at rest   O when they are in flight

5. **Where** do both butterflies and moths emerge from?

    O the bark of trees   O cocoons

6. **What** other traits do butterflies and moths have in common?

    O they both have antenna   O they both have colorful wings

Name: _____   Date: _____

Skateboarding

The first skateboard was created by a California surfer back in the 1950s. He attached roller skate wheels to a piece of wood that resembled a small surfboard so that he could surf on land as well as on the ocean.

Since then, skateboarding has become a sport, an art form, and a speedy mode of transportation. Today, many young people compete in skateboarding competitions, where they show off their skills and special tricks. Some cities, however, post "No Skateboarding" signs in certain areas where there is high pedestrian traffic so that no one gets injured. The fastest stand-up speed recorded on a skateboard was clocked at 55 miles per hour. In many places, that's the freeway speed limit for cars! In some places, skateboarders are issued citations for skating too fast on public sidewalks and streets.

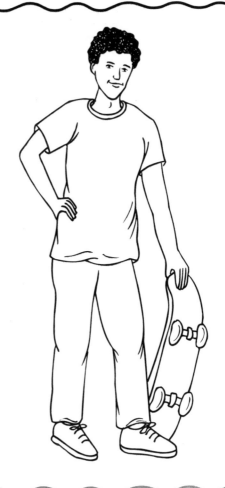

1. **When** was the first skateboard created?

    O in the 1960s   O in the 1950s   O in the 1970s

2. **Who** created the first skateboard?

    O a surfer   O a roller skater   O a car factory

3. **Who** competes in skateboarding competitions?

    O pedestrians   O young people   O surfers

4. **Where** might "No Skateboarding" signs be posted?

    O at competitions   O on freeways   O in pedestrian traffic areas

5. **What** is the fastest clocked stand-up skateboarding speed?

    O 65 MPH   O 55 MPH   O 25 MPH

Name: _____   **Date:** _____

If you have a lot of information to sort through, get organized! Classifying and categorizing are great ways to do this.

Directions: *The Word Box contains items specifically related to each of the occupations below. Match and fill in the puzzle.*

ACROSS
3. biologist
7. dentist
8. surgeon
12. carpenter
13. nurse
14. firefighter
15. gardener
16. farmer

DOWN
1. cook
2. tailor
4. accountant
5. singer
6. plumber
9. musician
10. programmer
11. painter

Word Box
thermometer
scalpel
chalk
grill
computer
tractor
drill
calculator
hose
wrench
microscope
brush
thread
trowel
trombone
hammer
microphone

Name: _____

Date: _____

Example: rabbit, dog, chicken, pig, mouse, whale, bear, monkey

Which does not belong with the rest? _____ chicken _____ *Why not?*

It is the only one that is not a mammal.

1. shampoo, sponge, towels, soap, rags, detergent, cleanser

   Which does not belong with the rest? _____

   Why not? _____

2. hut, tent, motel, cabin, nest, igloo, apartment, barn, house

   Which does not belong with the rest? _____

   Why not? _____

3. milk, cough syrup, olive oil, juice, cider, yogurt, water

   Which does not belong with the rest? _____

   Why not? _____

4. desk, table, bookshelves, lamp, pencil, chair, door

   Which does not belong with the rest? _____

   Why not? _____

5. ham, lettuce, turkey, cheese, peanut butter, tomato, soup, tuna

   Which does not belong with the rest? _____

   Why not? _____

6. hoe, rake, screwdriver, trowel, stakes, seeds, watering can, fertilizer

   Which does not belong with the rest? _____

   Why not? _____

Name: _____   **Date:** _____

Directions: *Your job below is to determine the relationship of what is being compared in each analogy and fill in the missing word.*

1. **piano** is to **keys** as **violin** is to _____ .

2. **circus** is to **clown** as **theater** is to _____ .

3. **horse** is to **gallop** as **eagle** is to _____ .

4. **mother** is to **woman** as **father** is to _____ .

5. **loud** is to **sound** as **sour** is to _____ .

6. **ant** is to **insect** as **Halloween** is to _____ .

7. **Pacific** is to **ocean** as **Saturn** is to _____ .

8. **strawberry** is to **fruit** as **daisy** is to _____ .

9. **cat** is to **kitten** as **dog** is to _____ .

10. **goose** is to **geese** as **mouse** is to _____ .

11. **clothes** are to **closet** as **car** is to _____ .

12. **ski** is to **snow** as **raft** is to _____ .

13. **grapes** are to **vine** as **lemon** is to _____ .

14. **roses** are to **florist** as **cakes** are to _____ .

15. **dune** is to **sand** as **mound** is to _____ .

Name: _____   **Date:** _____

1. *fry pan* is to *hamburger* as *kettle* is to _____
   steak   oyster   chili

2. *three* is to *nine* as *four* is to _____
   nine   twelve   six

3. *study* is to *learn* as *work* is to _____
   success   fun   revise

4. *pour* is to *drink* as *cook* is to _____
   fry   eat   restaurant

5. *intelligent* is to *brilliant* as *star* is to _____
   bright   super star   dull

6. *she* is to *her* as *he* is to _____
   him   they   men

7. *eat* is to *ate* as *sleep* is to _____
   slept   sleeping   awake

8. *cygnet* is to *swan* as *lamb* is to _____
   fowl   sheep   fawn

9. *apple* is to *fruit* as *zucchini* is to _____
   food   vegetable   bread

10. *eyelashes* are to *eyes* as *pages* are to _____
    books   libraries   computers

11. *pizza* is to *Italian* as *eggrolls* are to _____
    French   Chinese   Italian

12. *cookbook* is to *chef* as *Bible* is to _____
    teacher   minister   doctor

13. *cinnamon* is to *spice* as *rosemary* is to _____
    vegetables   pepper   herb

14. *snow* is to *white* as *blood* is to _____
    blue   scarlet   black

15. *pleasure* is to *smile* as *pain* is to _____
    suffer   grimace   tranquil

16. *native* is to *alien* as *nearby* is to _____
    odd   remote   stranger

17. *beautiful* is to *handsome* as *svelte* is to _____
    lean   ugly   attractive

18. *rural* is to *soil* as *urban* is to _____
    pavement   city   apartment

Name: _____   Date: _____

Directions: *Read each statement. Then, categorize each statement by writing FACT or OPINION on the line below.*

FACT:	**OPINION:**
There are thousands of kinds of fish.	Salt-water fish are the most beautiful.

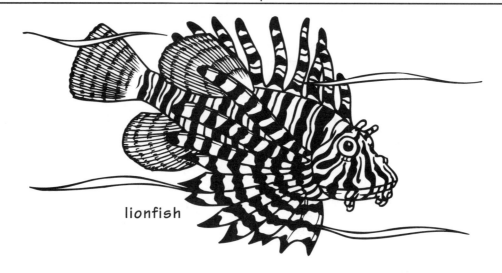

lionfish

1. Fish have fins and scales, and breathe through gills.

   _____

2. Keeping fish in an aquarium is an interesting hobby.

   _____

3. The Black Swallower can eat a fish larger than itself.

   _____

4. The poisonous lionfish is the most fascinating type of fish.

   _____

5. It is important to protect the habitats of fish.

   _____

6. Fish is an important part of the diet of many of the world's people.

   _____

7. Ichthyology is the scientific study of fish.

   _____

8. It would be great to be able to swim like a fish.

   _____

Name: _____   **Date:** _____

hemisphere
Europe
endangered species
territory
unconstitutional

interest rate
cartographer
isthmus
multiplication
parallel circuit

compass rose
transpiration
legislature
Civil War
static electricity

carnivore
centimeter
veto
right angle
percentage

Math Words	**Science Words**	**Measurement Words**
_____	_____	_____
_____	_____	_____
_____	_____	_____
_____	_____	_____
_____		

Social Studies Words	**Geography Words**
_____	_____
_____	_____
_____	_____
_____	_____

Name: _____   **Date:** _____

About 1,000 varieties of bats exist. Although they make up nearly one-quarter of all mammal species, few people have ever seen a bat because they are nocturnal, meaning they are most active during the night. During the day, bats often sleep upside down in roosts they create in caves and other structures.

Bats have furry bodies, sharp claws, sharp teeth, and wings. They are the only mammals capable of flight. Their leather-like wings allow them to swoop through the darkness in search of insects and moths.

Although many bats are insectivores, or insect eaters, many also dine on fruit, pollen, reptiles, fish, and small animals.

Bats find their way through the darkness by making high-pitched squeaks and clicks. The sounds they make bounce off nearby objects enabling them to sense the size, distance, and direction of the object based on the return of echoes. This is called ultrasonic echolocation. Because of this ability, it is said that bats have the most acute hearing of any terrestrial animal.

Diet	**Body Parts**
_____	_____
_____	_____
_____	_____
_____	_____
_____	**Special Characteristics**
_____	_____
_____	_____
	_____
	_____

Reading Comprehension • Saddleback Publishing, Inc. ©2002 3 Watson, Irvine, CA 92618•Phone (888)SDL-BACK•www.sdlback.com

1. A Galapagos tortoise's shell is very difficult to penetrate.

_____

2. These tortoises were named after a group of islands.

_____

3. The Galapagos Islands are in the Pacific Ocean.

_____

4. People introduced a dangerous predator to the islands.

_____

5. The Galapagos Islands are a part of Ecuador.

_____

6. The Galapagos tortoise is an endangered animal.

_____

7. The Galapagos tortoise was almost wiped out by natural causes.

_____

8. Today their numbers are increasing.

_____

Endangered Giant

How could an animal that weighs 330-440 pounds and is armored with a virtually impenetrable shell be in danger of becoming extinct?

Once thousands of these huge land-dwelling reptiles lived on a group of islands about 650 miles west of Ecuador in South America. So plentiful were they that the islands were named *Galapagos*, the Spanish word for *tortoise*.

In the early to middle 1800s, the Galapagos Islands were a popular stop for whaling and other ships. The tortoises not only provided a large amount of meat, but they were also easy to capture. It is estimated that between 1811 and 1844, more than 15,000 Galapagos tortoises were caught and taken aboard ships as food.

This was not the tortoises' only problem. Rats from the ships came ashore and preyed on the eggs and hatchlings.

In 1959, the government of Ecuador took steps to protect these humongous but gentle creatures from disappearing forever.

Name: _____　　**Date:** _____

Got two things to comprehend at the same time? A good way to examine them is by seeing how they are alike and different—compare and contrast.

Directions: *Read the topic sentence of each paragraph about seed plants. Then write A or B in front of each detail below to show in which paragraph it belongs.*

(A)

More than half of all seed plants are those that produce seeds in flowers.

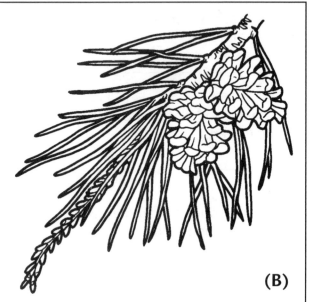

(B)

Conifers are like flowering plants in that they produce seeds, but conifers produce seeds in cones.

☐ Along with the colorful garden plants are many types of trees.

☐ These plants include pines, firs, spruces, hemlocks, and cedars.

☐ Fruits and vegetables, such as apples, lemons, and beans, are flowering plants.

☐ Most cones are hard, brown, and scaly.

☐ The seeds develop inside the base of the flower.

☐ The seeds are protected by the scales of the cones.

☐ Most flowering plants have broad leaves.

☐ These trees have either needles or scalelike leaves.

☐ Many are called evergreens because they stay green year-round.

☐ In general, flowering plants and trees lose their leaves at the end of the season.

Name: _____   **Date:** _____

(A)

The Shetland pony came from the Shetland Islands of Great Britain. It is the smallest of all horses, standing only 32-46 inches high. People originally used these stocky animals to pull coal carts. Later, they were imported into the United States as pets. They were later bred with the Hackney pony to produce a lighter, showier breed. Though still kept as pets, they are intelligent animals and must be trained by experts to be suitable for children.

(B)

The Shetland sheep dog was bred in the Shetland Islands for herding small livestock. It looks something like a miniature collie. Standing only 13-16 inches high, it doesn't seem like an animal that would be well-suited for the long, hard work of herding, but it has proved to be very rugged. The Shetland also has a more gentle nature than many other larger herding breeds, making it suitable as a pet.

_____ 1. Were originally bred in the Shetland Islands of Great Britain

_____ 2. Are small compared to other breeds

_____ 3. Is less than two feet tall

_____ 4. Must be trained to be suitable around children

_____ 5. Can and are kept as pets

_____ 6. Was used for herding small livestock

_____ 7. Has a more gentle nature than others of its type

_____ 8. Was first used to pull coal carts

Name: _____ **Date:** _____

Hey, you don't always have to be the one to answer questions about what you read. Sometimes it's helpful to ask your own questions.

Directions: *Read each ad carefully. Write a question that asks for some important detail that is missing. The example will get you started.*

A good "For Sale" classified ad should include

- the name of the object offered for sale
- a general description of it
- some specific features, if possible
- its age or condition
- the asking price
- a way of contacting the seller

Example: *Bike for sale. 10-speed. Boys. Red, with rack. Call 443-1203*

Q: How much does it cost? _____

1. Free to good home. Kittens, 10 weeks old. Adorable. Various colors.

Q: _____

2. Computer, with color monitor. $450 for both. E-Mail Ken at kennyd.com.

Q: _____

3. Great for student. Comes with chair. 1 year old. Only $35. 657-3390

Q: _____

4. Adult size Summit-Run™ Skis. Used once. Call Margo at 563-1298.

Q: _____

5. Mattress and box springs. Like new. Both for just $85. Won't last. 683-3415

Q: _____

6. Used car. Runs well. Needs new tires. $2,500. Call David's Auto at 763-4277.

Q: _____

Name: _____   **Date:** _____

1. In one word, what is Paragraph 1 about? _____

    Paragraph 2? _____

2. In general does a list give the main idea or a detail? _____

3. Write one detail given in Paragraph 2. _____

    _____

4. In which paragraph is the main idea (topic sentence) not the first sentence?

    _____

5. Write a question that could be answered by reading Paragraph 1.

    _____

6. Write a question that could be answered by reading Paragraph 2.

    _____

Good Stuff

Many varieties of sausage are available, each with a unique flavor. Sausage is meat that is chopped and seasoned, then stuffed into a casing. The meat may be any kind, such as beef, pork, veal, chicken, or even fish. It can be spiced with seasonings such as salt, pepper, sage, garlic, ginger, onions, or herbs. Sausage is sold raw for cooking and pre-cooked or smoked—ready to eat.

The frankfurter, or hotdog, is the most well known and popular type of sausage. It was named after the city of Frankfurt, Germany, but has become an American icon. Hotdogs are practically guaranteed to be on the menu at sporting events, amusement parks, and backyard cookouts all over the country.

Isn't it fun to guess what's going to come next in a story? Prediction is a good way to keep you focused on your reading and check your understanding. Try it.

Directions: *Use the clues in each statement to draw the conclusion of what it probably is.*

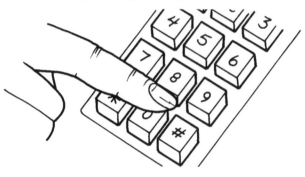

1. It has numbered push-buttons and an antenna.

   It is probably
   O a calculator.
   O a cellular phone.
   O a portable TV.

2. It is fluffy, white, hot, and comes in a bag.

   It is probably
   O clouds.
   O cotton.
   O popcorn.

3. It is soft, furry, and purrs when you feed it.

   It is probably
   O a rabbit.
   O a cat.
   O a stuffed animal.

4. It is smooth, sweet, creamy, and delicious hot or cold.

   It is probably
   O ice cream.
   O cheese.
   O pudding.

5. It is made of hard enamel encasing pulp and dentin.

   It is probably
   O a cup.
   O nail polish.
   O a tooth.

6. It can be long or short, and straight, wavy, or curly.

   It is probably
   O hair.
   O a road.
   O a river.

7. It has four legs and a soft body inside a hard shell.

   It is probably
   O an octopus.
   O a snail.
   O a turtle.

8. It is a few inches long, flat, and has many teeth for untangling.

   It is probably
   O a piranha.
   O a comb.
   O a saw.

9. It is orange, pointy, hard, and crunchy.

   It is probably
   O a pencil.
   O a carrot.
   O a marker.

Name: _____   **Date:** _____

1. My dog injured his foot, so...

_____

2. The woman got a parking ticket, so...

_____

3. The car was in the repair shop, so...

_____

4. Grandpa has trouble walking, so...

_____

5. We needed a loan to buy a car, so...

_____

6. It snowed all night last night, so...

_____

7. My brother wanted a goldfish, so...

_____

8. Mom had some books to return, so...

_____

• he ran home.	• we waited by the door.
• we went to the bank.	• we went to the pet store.
• he uses a cane.	• school was closed today.
• we took the bus to the mall.	• we took him to the vet.
• she had to pay a fine.	• she went to the library.

1. On board were 50 men with trinkets and treasures intended for trading with the native peoples when they disembarked.

   Where were the men?

   _____

2. The detective had that eerie feeling that sometimes comes over you when you walk among headstones...like a cold shiver.

   Where was the detective?

   _____

3. "Oh," said Sally, "I love the flat ones with the bows...but the pair with little heels are nice, too. Which should I get?"

   Where was Sally?

   _____

4. "They said this thing sleeps four," said Ben, "but our three sleeping bags are tight. At least open the flap and let some air in, Ed."

   Where were Ben and Ed?

   _____

5. "Shh! No noise in here!" Tia was scolded. She put her book up in front of her face until Mrs. Willis went behind another stack.

   Where was Tia?

   _____

Name: _____   **Date:** _____

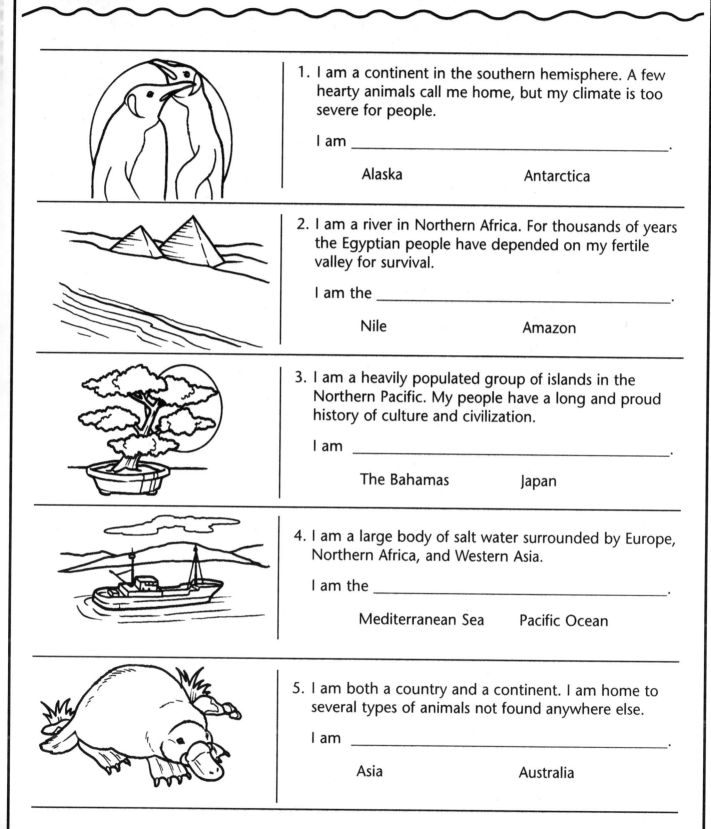

1. I am a continent in the southern hemisphere. A few hearty animals call me home, but my climate is too severe for people.

   I am _____.

   Alaska   Antarctica

2. I am a river in Northern Africa. For thousands of years the Egyptian people have depended on my fertile valley for survival.

   I am the _____.

   Nile   Amazon

3. I am a heavily populated group of islands in the Northern Pacific. My people have a long and proud history of culture and civilization.

   I am _____.

   The Bahamas   Japan

4. I am a large body of salt water surrounded by Europe, Northern Africa, and Western Asia.

   I am the _____.

   Mediterranean Sea   Pacific Ocean

5. I am both a country and a continent. I am home to several types of animals not found anywhere else.

   I am _____.

   Asia   Australia

Name: _____   Date: _____

Reading can be like solving a puzzle. Sometimes information is purposely not stated and left for you to figure out. Clues are given to help you fill in the holes.

Directions: *Read each quote. Decide who would most likely being saying it.*

librarian
grocery buyer
computer technician
horse trainer
science teacher
book salesperson
English teacher
police officer
farmer
mechanic
book illustrator
bank teller
dog trainer
firefighter
accountant
chemist

1. "I'd better get this field plowed before the rains come."

_____

2. "Sir, you were going 10 mph over the limit. May I see your license?"

_____

3. "Would you like to deposit this into your checking or savings account?"

_____

4. "There will be a quiz on Friday covering the chapter on weather."

_____

5. "The problem is that the power cord from the monitor is not working."

_____

6. "We're having a sale on mysteries. May I help you find a title or author?"

_____

7. "This breed is especially good with young children in the house."

_____

Name: _____   **Date:** _____

1. If penguins are found only in the southern hemisphere, then

   O all penguins are birds.

   O no penguins live in Alaska.

   O they share habitats with walrus.

2. If Maria brushes and flosses her teeth every day, then

   O she'll never get a cavity.

   O she won't need to see a dentist.

   O she is taking care of her teeth.

3. If Dan is a vegetarian and Mike is not, then

   O Dan will not eat meat.

   O Mike and Dan eat vegetables.

   O Mike will only eat meat.

4. If Jim has a mother cat and four kittens and two are male, then

   O two of Jim's cats are female.

   O Jim's cats all look alike.

   O he has more females than males.

5. If a 90% chance of rain is predicted for tomorrow, then

   O it will rain tomorrow.

   O it probably won't rain tomorrow.

   O it is likely to rain tomorrow.

6. If Janet has two sisters and one is older and the other younger, then

   O they have the same parents.

   O Janet is the middle child.

   O Janet has no brothers.

7. If Cole's house is north of Main and Rick's house north of Cole's, then

   O Rick lives south of Cole.

   O Main is south of Rick's and Cole's.

   O Main runs between their houses.

8. If our sun is the star nearest earth and it is 96 million miles away, then

   O all other stars are farther away.

   O other stars are close to the sun.

   O Saturn is closer than the sun.

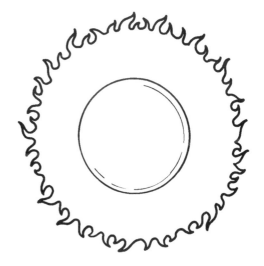

1. 1998 red, 2-door, automatic, leather interior, with bedliner. $9,800

   _____

2. White, side-by-side, with icemaker, 18 cubic feet. $400 OBO.

   _____

3. Full 26-volume set, hardcover, fully illustrated, published in late 90s.

   _____

4. Only 3 years old! Comes with 4 MB hard drive, plus monitor, keyboard, and loads of software. Must sacrifice at $650.

   _____

5. Adorable, cuddly, multicolored—6 in all. Have shots. Free to good home.

   _____

6. Assorted sizes from newborn to 18 mo. Jumpers, sleepwear, and accessories. Toys also available. Make offer.

   _____

7. Complete service for 8, includes extra spoons and serving pieces. $50

   _____

television
pickup truck
baby items
set of encyclopedias
stuffed animals
set of silverware
mattress
refrigerator
car
doll clothes
kittens
computer
set of model cars
set of dishes

Name: _____   **Date:** _____

The Many Faces of Spiders

Few of us have ever had the opportunity to observe a spider up close enough to see the details of its face. Though they can look very different from species to species, most spiders have certain features in common. _____

_____

A spider's eyes are near the front of its head. The size, number, and position of the eyes vary. Most have eight, arranged in two rows of four. _____

_____

_____. Just below the eyes and above the mouth are the chelicera, which end in hard, pointed claws that serve as fangs. _____

_____

The poison paralyzes or kills the prey. Certain spiders use their chelicera for other purposes as well. _____

_____. Others use their chelicera to dig burrows for nests.

Wolf Spider	Tarantula	Ogre-Faced Stick Spider
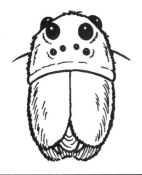		

- Spiders have eight legs, but insects have only six.
- But some have six, four, two, or none at all!
- Only those who live in the dark have no eyes.
- The fangs are used to inject poison.
- In most spiders the legs have claws, too.
- They have eyes, appendages called chelicera, and fangs.
- Some use them to crush their victims.

Want to get the most out of what you read? First preview it by scanning for key words or ideas and predict what you think the passage is about. Then read it carefully.

Directions: *Below are two pages from the table of contents of a health textbook. Use it to conclude if or where you could find in this book the information asked for.*

1. Industry is a major source of pollution. On what page(s) might you find information about this?

_____

2. Some foods have little or no nutritional value. In what chapter and section can you find out about these "empty" foods? _____

3. No listing is given for information about noise pollution. Under what topic(s) might it be found?

_____

4. On what pages will you find a guide to good nutrition? _____

5. Where can you find the name of the tube that leads from your mouth to your stomach?

_____

6. Where might there be information about landfills? _____

7. Does this book contain information about: a) dieting for people who are overweight? _____

   b) reusing paper and plastic products? _____

Name: _____   **Date:** _____

1. "Goldilocks and the Three Bears"

O Bears' Home Invaded By Stranger
O Girl Wakes Up In Strange Bed
O Bears Surprised By Little Girl

_____

_____

_____

2. "The Ugly Duckling"

O Duck Discovers He's A Swan
O Unusual Duck Born At Pond
O Duck Runs Away From Home

_____

_____

_____

3. "The Shoemaker and the Elves"

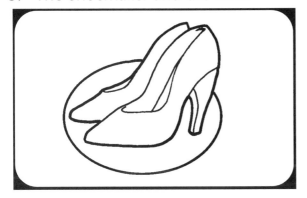

O Man Awakened By Strange Tapping
O Elves Save Shoemaker's Business
O Man Surprised By Shoes

_____

_____

_____

4. "The Emperor's New Clothes"

O Vain King Orders Suit
O Cloth Claimed To Be Magic
O King Embarrassed In Public

_____

_____

_____

Name: _____ **Date:** _____

Nicole studied the picture and wrote the statements below. Put a ✓ by the statements that are facts that can be concluded from the picture alone, not through her opinions or prior knowledge.

☐ The girl knows how to read.

☐ The girl is writing a diary.

☐ The scene takes place in the past.

☐ It is a warm summer day.

☐ The woman is the girl's mother.

☐ The people live on a farm.

☐ The girl is eleven years old.

☐ There are rain clouds in the distance.

☐ The dog is a family pet.

☐ The family is happy.

☐ The house has a fireplace.

☐ The girl has no shoes to wear.

Name: _____   **Date:** _____

Directions: Read both articles, then write V (Venus), M (Mars), or B (Both) on the blanks below.

Venus

Venus is our nearest planet neighbor. Viewed through a telescope, all that we can see is a thick blanket of yellow clouds. For years scientists wondered what might lie beneath those clouds—could the surface of Venus be like Earth?

The first probe was sent to Venus in the 1960s, and others followed. The initial data we got back was that the surface temperature reaches 890°F! Later we learned that the yellow cloud cover contains deadly sulfuric acid and the atmosphere is so thick, it would be like looking through soup. It may be the planet "next door" but Venus is hardly Earth-like.

Mars

Unlike Venus, the features of Mars are more like those of Earth—there are mountains, plains, canyons, and volcanoes. Mars has seasons and an atmosphere (though very thin). So, could there be life like ours on Mars?

In the 1970s the first probes landed on Mars. They let us know that: there is no carbon dioxide (necessary for life as we know it), there were only traces of water (not enough to support life), and there is almost no oxygen in the atmosphere (the part we need to breathe). It seems our neighbor, the red planet, has no residents we know of.

_____ 1. Has surface features similar to Earth's

_____ 2. The planet closest in distance to Earth

_____ 3. Could not support life as we know it

_____ 4. Has a very thick atmosphere

_____ 5. Was probed for information

_____ 6. Surface features can be seen through a telescope

_____ 7. Has known traces of water

_____ 8. Has an atmosphere

Name: _____   **Date:** _____

(A)

_____ 1. More than 68,000 boxes of cotton candy were sold during that fair.

_____ 2. This was possible because of the invention of an electric candy machine, patented that year.

_____ 3. What we know as cotton candy was introduced at the 1904 World's Fair.

(B)

_____ 1. Johnny Appleseed was a legendary folk hero.

_____ 2. He spent his life traveling about the countryside spreading apple seeds.

_____ 3. He is often pictured with a sack and a long-handled tin pan on his head.

(C)

_____ 1. The two who achieved this feat were Robert Peary and Matthew Henson.

_____ 2. Their success generated world-wide interest in polar exploration.

_____ 3. In 1909 the first explorers reached the North Pole.

(D)

_____ 1. The term is believed to have been first used about 1863 in reference to Dolly Madison.

_____ 2. The wife of the president of the United States is called the First Lady.

_____ 3. Some "first ladies" hold prominent places in history in their own right.

Jackie Kennedy

Shields

Until firearms came along, the main protection in a confrontation was the shield. The concept, still in use today, was to place a barrier between yourself and the threat. The shield was designed to be held in front with one hand, leaving the other hand free. The shield could be moved up and down to shield the head or legs, or in some cases, crouched behind to conceal the holder.

The earliest people made shields from wood. The shields were sometimes covered with animal hide. Later, metal shields appeared. Their primary purpose was self-defense. Shields were developed in a variety of shapes. A large round shield called a *clipeus* was used by the Greeks and Romans. The Romans also used a rectangular shield and developed an oblong variety called a *scutum*. During the Middle Ages, shields were decorated with coats of arms and other symbols.

1. Metal was the first material used to make shields.

   _____

2. Today's police use shields made from hard plastic.

   _____

3. Early Greeks and Romans used a variety of shields.

   _____

4. A clipeus was a rectangular-shaped shield.

   _____

5. Early hunters fooled their prey by hiding behind shields covered in animal skins.

   _____

6. Shields were effective against rocks, spears, and swords.

   _____

7. The invention of firearms made shields obsolete.

   _____

8. Shields could be held in either hand.

   _____

Main Idea: _____

_____

_____

_____

Name: _____

Date: _____

- They usually construct a web in an open area where there is likely to be bug "traffic."

- These spiders generally have bodies that are large relative to their legs.

- The group of spiders known as orb spiders are named for the type of web they spin—round, or orb-shaped.

- When finished with the web, the spider waits for an unsuspecting meal to fly into its sticky trap.

- Orb spiders depend entirely on their web to catch prey.

_____

_____
_____
_____
_____
_____
_____
_____
_____
_____
_____
_____
_____
_____
_____

Name: _____   **Date:** _____

An Honor

The Newbery Medal is an award given annually by The American Library Association to an author for the most distinguished contribution to children's literature published in the preceding year. The award is named after John Newbery, an English publisher and bookseller, who, in the 1700s, was among the first to put children's books in print.

The Newbery Award was established in 1921 by Frederic G. Melcher, then chairman of the board of the *Library Journal* and *Publisher's Weekly*. Mr. Melcher also established the Caldecott Medal, a similar award recognizing an outstanding illustrator of children's books.

You probably recognize or have read some Newbery award winners—old and new—such as Carol Ryrie Brink's *Caddie Woodlawn* (1936), Madeleine L'Engle's *A Wrinkle in Time* (1963), Robert C. O'Brien's *Mrs. Frisby and the Rats of NIMH* (1972), Patricia MacLachlan's *Sarah, Plain and Tall* (1986) or even the 2001 winner, Richard Peck's *A Year Down Yonder*.

Main Idea: _____

_____

1. What award is given to a distinguished author of children's literature?
   - O Newbery Medal
   - O Caldecott Medal

2. Who established the Newbery Award?
   - O John Newbery
   - O Frederic G. Melcher

3. How often is the Newbery Medal awarded?
   - O once a year
   - O twice a year

4. If the award was given in the year 1998, in what year was the book published?
   - O 1998
   - O 1997

5. What are the *Library Journal* and *Publisher's Weekly*?
   - O books
   - O magazines

6. Who awards the Newbery Medal?
   - O American Library Association
   - O Frederic G. Melcher

7. Where did children's books first appear in print?
   - O England
   - O United States

8. The Caldecott Medal is awarded to an outstanding
   - O writer
   - O artist

Name: _____ **Date:** _____

Although they look similar, a hare is not a rabbit. There are several distinctions.

First, hares are larger than rabbits. They also have longer ears and much longer back legs. Next, unlike rabbits, hares generally live alone. They do not burrow like rabbits, but rather lay in grass in what is called "forms"—indentations that keep the form of the animal. Like rabbits, hares come in a wide range of colors.

Baby hares are called leverets. Unlike bunnies, they are born with their eyes open and can use their powerful legs very soon after they are born.

1. *Which sentence best states the main idea of the story?*

   O Hares look like rabbits.
   O Hares have longer ears than rabbits.
   O Hares and rabbits share many characteristics.
   O Hares and rabbits have distinct differences.

2. *Which would be the best title for this story?*

   O The Solitary Hare   O All in the Rabbit Family
   O Don't Call Me a Rabbit   O Bunnies and Leverets

3. *Reread these sentences in the story.*
   Choose the one that does not belong.

   O Like rabbits, hares come in a wide variety...
   O There are several distinctions.
   O They do not burrow like rabbits...
   O Baby hares are called leverets.

4. *Which of these is <u>not</u> a conclusion you can draw from the passage?*

   O Baby rabbits are called bunnies.
   O Hares are often mistakenly called rabbits.
   O Rabbits and hares come in different colors.
   O Baby hares are less dependent at birth than baby rabbits.

Shooting Stars

1. What do we see in the sky today that is different from what early people saw?

   _____

2. Is "shooting star" an accurate name for the streaks of light we sometimes observe in the night sky? _____ Why or why not?

   _____

   _____

3. What is the name of a chunk of debris from space that reaches and hits the Earth's surface?

   _____

4. What enables us to see a meteor?

   _____

   _____

5. Could you ever see a meteorite? _____ If so, how; if not, why?_____

   _____

6. Which of the following occurs most frequently—meteorites, meteors, or meteoroids? _____

7. What is the main idea of the story? _____

   _____

When early people gazed at the sky, they saw the same things we do—the sun, the moon, and the stars. Sometimes they saw streaks of light shooting across the sky. Even today we call these shooting stars, but we know that they are not stars at all. Shooting stars are actually meteors— debris from space that has entered the earth's atmosphere. The friction causes the rock and metal to heat up and glow. As it moves, we see it as a streak of light.

Where do meteors come from? Meteors begin as meteoroids—chunks of rock or metal traveling through space. They can't be seen until they enter our atmosphere. Then they become meteors and we can see their trails.

Do meteors ever reach the Earth's surface? Yes! A meteor that lands on the surface is called a meteorite. Most are so small that you could mistake them for ordinary rocks. But every so often a substantial meteorite strikes. If it is large enough, the impact causes a crater.

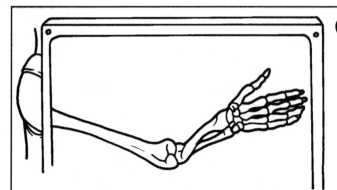

(A) Have you ever had an X ray taken? If you have had a broken bone, toothache, or taken a suitcase on an airplane you probably have. At the dentist you put the film inside your mouth. An X ray is a special way to take a picture of a bone, tooth, or object concealed from direct sight.

(B) X rays are useful in many ways. By reading an X ray, a doctor can see if a bone is broken or if a tooth has a cavity. The X ray process was discovered in 1895. X rays are useful in finding other hidden things, too. For example, bags at an airport are X rayed to see if any dangerous items are inside without having to open and look in each one.

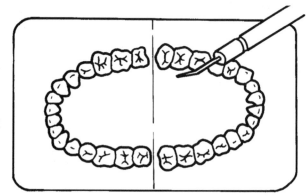

1. Copy the sentence in Paragraph A that gives the main idea.

    _____

    _____

2. Cross out one sentence in each paragraph that gives a detail that does not belong in the paragraph.

3. Explain why the sentence you crossed out in Paragraph A does not belong.

    _____

    _____

4. Explain why the sentence you crossed out in Paragraph B does not belong.

    _____

    _____

5. Write a good title for the story.

    _____

Name: _____   **Date:** _____

FYI

An *acronym* is a word formed by the first or first few letters of a series of words. Acronyms are seen and recognized in many forms. For example, the title of this passage is an acronym for *For Your Information*. Other acronyms you may be familiar with are *ASAP—As Soon As Possible* and *BLT—Bacon, Lettuce, and Tomato*. A *palindrome* is a word spelled the same forward and backward, such as peep.

Some acronyms are so common that you may not even know what words they came from. For example, the ZIP in your ZIP code stands for *Zone Improvement Plan*, your IQ is your *Intelligence Quotient*, and if you get E-mail on your PC, it's *Electronic Mail* on your *Personal Computer*.

1. What is the main idea of the passage? _____

   _____

2. Which sentence does not belong in the passage? _____

   _____

3. Why is the title appropriate for the passage? _____

   _____

4. What are some examples of acronyms? _____

   _____

5. If you ride in an SUV you are in a Sport Utility Vehicle. Is this an acronym?

   Why or why not? _____

   _____

6. The following words are not acronyms. Why? VET, MATH, GYM, BURGER, FLU

   _____

Name: _____   Date: _____

Do you ever feel as if you need a map to keep you on track with something you are reading or writing? An outline is kind of like a map that you can follow.

Directions: *Read the article. Then, examine each paragraph and fill in the outline below. Use the back of this page as needed.*

Dolls of the New World

No one knows how or where the first dolls were created—they seem to be a part of many cultures, old and new. When Europeans first came to America, they found that the native peoples had many kinds of dolls. Dolls were made for teaching, for ceremonies, for representing important ideas, and just for play. Dolls were made from animal skins, cornhusks, and grass. They were stuffed with moss, animal hair, or dried grass. They were adorned with beads, shells, and seeds.

As Europeans began to settle in the new land, their dolls came with them. William Penn, for whom the state of Pennsylvania is named, brought a doll from England in 1699 for a friend of his daughter, Letitia. Other dolls were brought from Europe, but soon the colonial children began making their own dolls. They were whittled from wood, or made from rags or cornhusks. Some were stuffed with sawdust and decorated with yarn, beads, lace, or other adornments.

Paragraph I (main idea) _____

   A. (supporting detail) _____

   B. (supporting detail) _____

   C. (supporting detail) _____

   D. (supporting detail) _____

Paragraph II (main idea) _____

   A. (supporting detail) _____

   B. (supporting detail) _____

   C. (supporting detail) _____

Name: _____   **Date:** _____

South America

South America is the fourth largest of the seven continents. The land is made up of mountains, plains, and tropical forest. Most of the population is concentrated in large coastal cities.

The continent of South America is rich in natural resources. Its chief agricultural exports are bananas, coffee, cocoa, sugar cane, and wool. Minerals such as gold, copper, and iron ore are also exported.

One of South America's outstanding natural features is the Amazon River basin. Covering an area of more than two million square miles, it is the largest drainage basin in the world. The river itself is nearly 4,000 miles long.

South America's vast tropical forests provide a lush haven for a variety of wildlife. The largest numbers and kinds of plant and animal life are found in and around the basin of the Amazon River. Many people around the world are concerned that South America's forests are being sacrificed at an alarming rate for human exploits.

Paragraph I (main idea) _____

   A. (supporting detail) _____

   B. (supporting detail) _____

Paragraph II (main idea) _____

   A. (supporting detail) _____

   B. (supporting detail) _____

Paragraph III (main idea) _____

   A. (supporting detail) _____

Paragraph IV (main idea) _____

   A. (supporting detail) _____

   B. (supporting detail) _____

Name: _____   **Date:** _____

Hey, you are smart but no one can remember every detail of what was read. That's why summarizing is so cool—just boil it down to the essential information.

Directions: *Read the passage and questions. Fill in the bubbles of the correct answers and write a brief summary of this article on the lines below. Use the back of this page as needed.*

Melanophia are a type of beetle with an amazing ability—they can sense the presence of fire. When a fire breaks out, melanophia can detect the blaze up to 30 miles away. Their larvae feed on freshly burnt wood, so melanophia rush to the scene where they lay their eggs in the charred timbers. Often as firefighters arrive, they find melanophia by the hundreds already there. Some firefighters report being bitten. Because of their attraction to and need for fire, melanophia are often called "fire beetles."

1. Which sentence best states the main idea of the story?

   O Melanophia beetles are sometimes called "fire beetles."
   O One type of beetle can sense the presence of fire.
   O The melanophia beetle can sense a blaze 30 miles away.
   O The melanophia beetle larvae feed on freshly burnt wood.

2. Which would be the best title for this story?

   O Six-Legged Firefighters   O The Amazing Melanophia
   O First on the Scene   O Fire Alarm

Summary: _____

_____

_____

_____

_____

_____

Name: _____   **Date:** _____

Everyone Loves a Bargain

In today's world it seems that everywhere we turn we see advertising—appeals for us to buy something—on TV, radio, billboards, signs, mailings, newspapers, and now the Internet. We are enticed to buy not only the things we need, but also things we didn't even know existed.

Do you ever wonder how people got the things they wanted or needed before all the marketing tools we have now were available? The answer is often they didn't. There were stores, but the owners bought small quantities of goods from traveling merchants. They made a guess at what their customers might want and put the merchandise in their stores. There was no enticement to draw customers in.

About 100 years ago, a shrewd businessman named Frank Woolworth had several odds and ends in his store that hadn't sold. He set up a table and marked it "Any Article on this table–5¢." In no time all, the "unwanted" merchandise was gone. Woolworth discovered that people love a bargain! He knew if he purchased large quantities of items he could get a lower price, then sell the items at a "bargain" to the customer. He established the very successful Woolworth's chain of stores and paved the way for today's department and discount stores.

Summary: _____

_____

_____

_____

_____

_____

_____

_____

_____

_____

Name: _____ **Date:** _____

Most people enjoy solving problems—it is what keeps life interesting. It's the same in stories. We enjoy seeing how characters solve the problems that come up.

Directions: *Read the story. Think about each question, then answer YES or NO. Finally, write what you think would be the best solution to Kenny's problem on the back of this page.*

Nora Stein arrived home from the hospital at the usual time—just before Kenny got home from school. But what she found when she got there was unusual!

Her favorite plant was knocked over—dirt spewed out on the carpet. The vase of flowers on the coffee table was overturned and the flowers destroyed. The rest of the room was fine—if you didn't count the rips in the curtains! And, Ignatius was nowhere to be found.

When Kenny walked in he saw the same thing, with one addition—Mom with "that" expression on her face. "Uh-oh," thought Kenny.

"Well, young man," said Nora. "It looks as if you forgot to put that iguana back in his cage when you left this morning."

Kenny spotted Ignatius sitting on top of the curtain rail. "Sorry, Mom," he said. Then silently he decided not to ask her if he could keep the snake he found on the way home.

1. Nora Stein is Kenny's mother.

_____

2. Nora was a patient at the hospital.

_____

3. Ignatius is Kenny's brother.

_____

4. Kenny did not put his pet away that morning.

_____

5. Nora works at the hospital.

_____

6. Nora was already at work when Kenny left in the morning.

_____

7. Ignatius has claws.

_____

8. Kenny knew what "that" look meant.

_____

9. Kenny changed his mind about asking if he could have a snake.

_____

Name: _____

Date: _____

October 17, 2002

Dear Abby,

Things just don't seem the same since you moved away last month. At school, Terry and I still eat lunch together, but it's not as much fun without you there, too. The other day while passing your old house on the way home from school, I noticed the new family has a golden retriever, just like your Bucky. For a minute it seemed as if you still lived here.

My mom talked to your mom and told me you might come back East during the winter break in December to visit your grandparents. I hope you do. Maybe they would bring you over from Collingsville to spend the night while you are here. Maybe we could even go skating at the rink like we used to. Terry could come, too.

Please write back and tell me how you like your new school and living in the desert. Does it snow in Arizona?

Your friend,
Liz

1. Who moved away?
   O Abby
   O Liz
   O Terry

2. When did the move occur?
   O October
   O December
   O September

3. Who is Bucky?
   O Abby's friend
   O the new family's dog
   O Abby's dog

4. Where do Abby's grandparents live?
   O Collingsville
   O the East
   O Arizona

5. Who could bring Abby to Liz's?
   O Abby's parents
   O Liz's parents
   O Abby's grandparents

6. What did Liz hope for most?
   O Abby to visit
   O to go skating
   O a golden retriever

7. What's the main problem mentioned in the letter?
   O Abby misses Liz.
   O Liz wants to come to Arizona.
   O Liz misses Abby.

8. How could this problem be solved?
   O Liz and Abby could get together for a visit on vacations.
   O Liz could move to Arizona to be closer to Abby.
   O Terry and Liz could forget Abby and make new friends at school.

Planet	Diameter	Time of Orbit	Time of Rotation	Distance from Sun	Surface Gravity
Earth	7,926 mi.	365 days	24 hours	96 mil. mi.	1.00
Venus	7,521 mi.	224 days	243 days	68 mil. mi.	.88

———————— 1. Venus has an atmosphere unlike Earth's.

———————— 2. Earth and Venus are very close in size.

———————— 3. Earth is closer to the sun than is Venus.

———————— 4. If you weigh 100 pounds on Earth, you would weigh 88 pounds on Venus.

———————— 5. It takes less time for Venus to go around the sun than it does for Earth.

———————— 6. Compared to Earth, Venus rotates very quickly.

———————— 7. You would weigh more on Venus than you would on the moon.

———————— 8. Venus can make one trip around the sun faster than it can rotate once.

———————— 9. From Earth, Venus is shrouded in a yellowish cloud cover.

———————— 10. It is approximately 28 million miles from Earth to Venus.

———————— 11. Earth makes one complete rotation on its axis every day.

———————— 12. Gravity is stronger on Venus than on Earth.

The **roots** of a plant serve several purposes. One is to anchor the plant into the soil. They also serve as probes for moisture and minerals. A third function is to absorb water and minerals and send it up to the **plant**. There are two main kinds of roots–the **primary root** and the **secondary roots**, which include hair roots.

Within the plant, fats and proteins are made by chemical changes in the sugars and starches. The **stem**, or trunk in the case of trees, is like a highway carrying supplies to the plant. It is through the **leaves** that carbon dioxide is absorbed and oxygen given off. It is also the job of the leaves to collect sunlight, which is needed to make food. Leaves are often flat so as to expose more surface area and seem to arrange themselves in ways that allow them to collect the light. Tendrils are wispy offshoots of the stem that reach up or out and may act as coils to attach the plant to something.

Finally, the **blossom** of a flowering plant is actually a seed factory. It uses the food the plant has produced to form seeds.

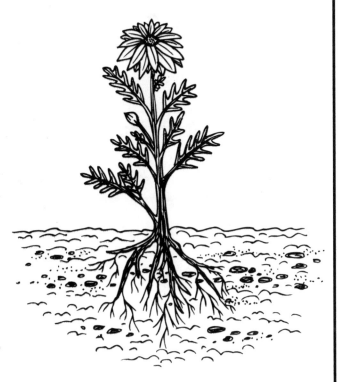

1. How does a plant breathe? _____

_____

2. How does a plant drink? _____

_____

3. How does a plant eat? _____

_____

GRADE A
PASTEURIZED

VITAMINS A & D

FAT FREE MILK

Nutrition Facts

Serv. Size 1 cup (240 ml.)
Servings about 16
Calories 90 Fat Cal. 0
*Percent Daily Values (DV) are based on a 2,000 calorie diet.

Amount/Serving	%DV*	Amount/Serving	%DV*
Total Fat 0g	0%	**Total Carb.** 13g	4%
Sat. Fat 0g	0%	Fiber 0g	0%
Cholest. less than 5mg	1%	Sugars 12g	
Sodium 130mg	5%	**Protein** 9g	18%
Vitamin A 10% • Vitamin C 4% • Calcium 36% • Vitamin D 25%			

INGREDIENTS: GRADE A FAT FREE MILK, VITAMIN A PALMIATE, VITAMIN D₃

Nutrition Facts

Serving Size 3 cookies (35g)
Servings Per Container About 7

Amount Per Serving

Calories 170 Calories from Fat 70

% Daily Value*

Total Fat 8g	**12%**
Saturated Fat 1g	**5%**
Cholesterol 0mg	**0%**
Sodium 105mg	**4%**
Total Carbohydrate 22g	**7%**
Dietary Fiber 1g	**4%**
Sugars 11g	
Protein 3g	

Vitamin A 0% • Vitamin C 0%
Calcium 0% • Iron 2%

1. George had three cookies. How many of the calories were from fat? _____

2. George had a 16-ounce glass of milk. A cup is 8 ounces. How many calories were in his big glass of milk? _____

3. Based on a 2,000-calorie diet, what percentage of his daily value of calcium did his big glass of milk provide? _____

4. How many grams of sugars did George have in his total snack? _____

5. George had 15 percent of his total carbohydrates needed for the day. How many grams of carbohydrates was that? _____

6. Did George's snack provide more or less than 1/4 of the recommended limit of sodium for the day? _____

7. Was George's snack low or high in cholesterol? _____

8. George likes to keep an eye on his weight. What was the total number of calories in his snack? _____

9. George drinks fat free milk, but the cookies had 8 grams of fat. What percentage of his recommended limit of fat did those three cookies take? _____

10. Based on the listing of total fat and saturated fat on the cookies, for which is the daily allowance lower? _____ About how many grams of saturated fat are allowed per day for a person with a 2,000-calorie diet? _____

Name: _____   **Date:** _____

Having a pet is fun. Is that a fact? Well, no, because some people may think so, but others do not. Recognizing fact and opinion is an important tool in reading and life!

Directions: *Each statement below is an opinion. Do you agree, disagree, or need more information to make a decision?*

Everyone has opinions. We form our opinions from what we see, hear, read, and share with others. We decide in our minds what we believe. We may or may not agree with someone else. And, sometimes we change our minds when we get new or different information.

1 Brand-name clothes and shoes are better than store brands.

- O agree
- O disagree
- O need more information

2. If you go to a dentist twice a year, you won't get any cavities.

- O agree
- O disagree
- O need more information

3. Hockey is more interesting than baseball.

- O agree
- O disagree
- O need more information

4. Division is harder to learn than multiplication.

- O agree
- O disagree
- O need more information

5. Someday people will live on the moon.

- O agree
- O disagree
- O need more information

6. The price of a movie ticket is too high.

- O agree
- O disagree
- O need more information

7. All children should get allowance for doing chores.

- O agree
- O disagree
- O need more information

8. To do your best you need at least eight hours of sleep.

- O agree
- O disagree
- O need more information

Name: _____

Date: _____

Directions: *Here is a tricky puzzle to solve. The answers to the puzzle are hidden in the clues. The tricky part is figuring out which word in the clue is the answer. It is the one that best signals that the sentence is an opinion. The first one is done for you.*

ACROSS

2. That's <u>enough</u> sugar.
4. This mattress is soft.
6. It's impossible for us to agree.
9. I think this is your problem.
10. Learning to multiply is easy.
11. Our team is great!

DOWN

1. He won't make it.
3. Pizza is delicious.
4. She should get the award.
5. I am going fast.
7. Your hair looks better short.
8. Living on a farm is fun.

Reading Comprehension • Saddleback Publishing, Inc. ©2002   3 Watson, Irvine, CA 92618•Phone (888)SDL-BACK• www.sdlback.com

(A) Fantasy

A fairy tale is a make-believe story that usually includes imaginary beings such as fairies, giants, or creatures. These folklore beings are seen by and talk to humans but often do things that involve magic. Some fairy tale beings are good, and some are bad, but a fairy tale often has a happy ending. Some examples are the stories of Cinderella, Rumpelstiltskin, and Tom Thumb. One of my favorites is Jack and the Beanstalk.

(B) Reality

A legend is a form of folklore that teaches lessons about life and may contain fanciful actions, but is based in reality. In fact, some of the characters or events may be rooted in truth, but exaggerated. A well-known example is the legend of King Arthur and his knights. Some of the things referred to in these tales are borne out in English history. My favorite legendary character is Robin Hood.

_____ 1. Fairy tales are based on real events.

_____ 2. To state a favorite story is an opinion.

_____ 3. Legends and fairy tales are forms of folklore.

_____ 4. Robin Hood is a legend.

_____ 5. The King Arthur stories take place in England.

_____ 6. Legends are historical fact.

_____ 7. All fairy tales have happy endings.

_____ 8. Fairy tales and legends are fiction stories.

Name: _____   **Date:** _____

Your brain is like a computer—you can delete things that add no useful or new information.

Directions: *Put a ✓ by each sentence that would belong in a story about the Harlem Globetrotters. Put a ✗ by each sentence that does not stick to the subject.*

☐ The Harlem Globetrotter team was founded by Abe Saperstein in 1927.

☐ Basketball and football are popular spectator sports.

☐ The Globetrotters have played in more than 100 countries.

☐ Their theme song is "Sweet Georgia Brown."

☐ It is difficult to spin a basketball on the tip of your finger.

☐ The Globetrotters scored 8,829 consecutive victories over 24 years.

☐ NBA stands for National Basketball Association.

☐ It took a team of retired NBA players to defeat them.

☐ Many basketball players are taller than average people.

☐ The players were known for their skill and fancy ball handling.

☐ The Globetrotters have also been called the "Ambassadors of Good Will."

☐ A basket is worth two points.

Name: _____   **Date:** _____

(A) The word *sphinx* refers to an imaginary creature that appears in ancient myths of Egypt and other cultures of the region. The features vary from story to story, but frequently describe the sphinx as having the head of a human, the body of a lion, the tail of a serpent, and the wings of a bird. The most famous sphinx is the Great Sphinx, which stands near the Great Pyramids in Egypt. The pyramids are very old. This sphinx has the head of a human and the body, legs, and tail of a lion. It does not have wings.

1. Underline the sentence that gives the main idea of the paragraph.

2. Cross out the sentence that gives a detail that does not belong.

3. Write true or false: *The sphinx is a purely Egyptian concept.* _____

(B) The area with the lowest elevation in the Western Hemisphere is known as Death Valley. The lowest spot lies 282 feet below sea level, but this region is not underwater—it is a desolate desert located in east-central California near the Nevada border. It gets only about 2 inches of rainfall a year, and in summer, temperatures of 120°F are common. Not many people live there. Death Valley seems like a harsh name for a place, but the pioneers who named it in the 1840s felt **it** was well deserved.

1. Underline the sentence that summarizes the main idea of the paragraph.

2. Cross out the sentence that gives a detail that does not belong.

3. What does the **boldfaced** word "it" refer to? Fill in the bubble below:

    O Death Valley   O name   O place

(A) Molting is the name given to the process an animal uses to shed its skin, feathers, hair, or body parts. In insects, as a larvae grows, the outer covering becomes too small. Snakes shed their skin for a similar reason. This may take only a few minutes. It is really weird to watch. Many species of birds shed their feathers, but unlike insects or snakes, this process is gradual. Mammals also replace their hair or fur over a long period. Perhaps the most dramatic case of molting occurs in deer and moose. They shed their antlers every spring.

1. Underline the sentence that gives the main idea.

2. Cross out the sentence that gives a detail that does not belong.

3. Write a good title: _____

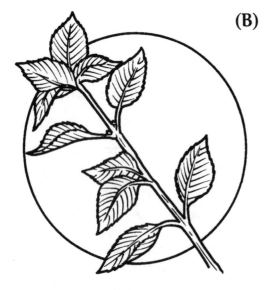

(B) When you hear the word mint, you may think of the flavor of peppermint. Peppermint is a pleasant flavor to many people. But mint is actually the name of a family of plants. Actually about 32,000 kinds of mint exist. Mint grows all over the world. The leaf and the oil are used for flavoring in foods and in producing scented products. Mint may also be used in some kinds of medicine. Some common mint plants are lavender, marjoram, rosemary, sage, thyme, spearmint, and of course, peppermint.

1. Underline the sentence that gives the main idea.

2. Cross out the sentence that gives a detail that does not belong.

3. Write a good title: _____

Name: _____   **Date:** _____

(A) (1) Parakeet is the name given to several small birds in the parrot family. (2) They usually roost in trees and are found in tropical areas of the world. (3) Parakeets are sometimes sold in pet stores. (4) Parakeets live in groups and feed on mainly seeds, fruit, flowers, and leaves.

I. Sentence (___) does not belong in this passage because _____

_____

_____

II. Read each statement. Circle True or False, then write the sentence number that supports your answer.

a. Parakeet are small types of parrots.	true	false	Sentence (___)
b. Parakeets are vegetarians.	true	false	Sentence (___)
c. Parakeets are found in every part of the world.	true	false	Sentence (___)

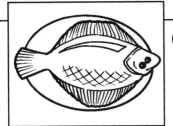

(B) (1) The flounder is a common fish with some uncommon characteristics. (2) Like many other fish, the flounder has a flat body, but rather than swim around, the flounder spends most of its time lying down! (3) Both eyes of this fish are on the same side of its body. (4) It can also change its color to match its surroundings, which is often the sandy or pebbly sea floor. (5) Camouflage is just one way some animals hide from their enemies.

I. Sentence (___) does not belong in this passage because _____

_____

_____

II. Read each statement. Circle True or False, then write the sentence number that supports your answer.

a. Flounder have an unusual-shaped body.	true	false	Sentence (___)
b. A flounder has no eyes on one of its sides.	true	false	Sentence (___)
c. Flounder are found in the ocean.	true	false	Sentence (___)

Name: _____ **Date:** _____

Directions: *Each passage is an excerpt from a different type of reading material. Identify it.*

manual	letter	schedule	recipe	textbook
newspaper	dictionary	thesaurus	novel	

1. April 4 FOUR RESCUED OFFSHORE
A small craft capsized last evening just off the shore near Teak Island...

   Joe is reading a

   _____.

2. **satisfy** *verb meaning to grant or have; supply fully;* synonyms: *appease, fulfill, answer, meet*

   Joe is reading a

   _____.

3. 6 PM **2 4 7** News (CC)
   (HIS) Modern Marvels 1:00
   (TLC) Ancient Prophecies 1:00
   (DIS) Rascal (G) HH Tale of a
           boy and a raccoon. 1:25

   Joe is reading a

   _____.

4. Dear Nana Helen,
   Today I received your card...

   Joe is reading a

   _____.

5. tripod /tri päd/ n [from Gr. tri (three) + pod (foot)] 1: a pot, stool, table that rests on three legs   2: three-legged stand for a camera

   Joe is reading a

   _____.

6. Suddenly the knight found himself face to face with an actual dragon. It was not as he had expected...

   Joe is reading a

   _____.

7. A dialog box appears. To select, click the name of the hard drive.

   Joe is reading a

   _____.

8. Combine dry ingredients in a separate bowl. Slowly add the melted chocolate, stirring continuously until well-blended.

   Joe is reading a

   _____.

Name: _____

Date: _____

1. Simone blinked a few times to make sure that what she saw was real—yes, it was what she thought it was—a fine white horse, but more than that. It did have the long spiral horn and beautiful feathered wings. Simone moved closer. The creature lowered its head and beckoned her forward.

This is _____.

I concluded this from _____

_____

_____

2. Derek Hall put on his uniform and looked in the mirror. The number on his jersey was backwards, but he reminded himself of what it meant— commitment to do your best. Last week he had let the team down by missing an easy goal. This week he was determined to redeem himself.

This is _____.

I concluded this from _____

_____

_____

3. Aeneas, having witnessed the stunning trick played at Troy, was determined to get his father out of the city. As it was being overrun, Aeneas, carrying his sick father on his back, escaped the burning city to a boat. Safe outside the city walls, they and a few other survivors traveled to a distant haven, Latium, later to become Rome.

This is _____.

I concluded this from _____

_____

_____

4. One of the most renown violinists of our time was Isaac Stern. Born in Russia in 1920, he was brought to America at the age of one. Amazingly, he made his musical debut with the San Francisco Symphony Orchestra at age 11! He went on to perform with the Los Angeles Philharmonic Orchestra and at Carnegie Hall.

This is _____.

I concluded this from _____

_____

_____

Here's a tip. Identifying the topic sentence is like asking, "What's it all about?"

Directions: *Read the questions below. Keep the topic sentence in mind as you read the story. Then go back and answer the questions.*

1. What is the topic sentence? _____

2. What secret did the Chinese keep? _____

3. What do silk farmers grow? _____

4. What word means a period of 1,000 years? _____

5. Did the Chinese make much money in the silk trade? _____

6. What do silkworms consume? _____

7. What word is the opposite of synthetic? _____

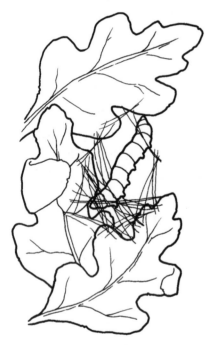

The Story of Silk

Silk cloth has been an expensive and prized material for thousands of years. At first, only the Chinese knew how to make silk, and they kept their secret for a very long time. Other nations sought the remarkable material, and China carried on a profitable trade for well over a millennium.

So what was the secret? Where did the Chinese get this treasured fiber that is stronger, lighter, and warmer than cotton, and which can be dyed to the richest of colors? The "thread" used to make silk cloth is actually made by worms! Silkworms spin the shiny fiber to form their cocoons. The silk is "harvested" by unravelling the cocoon. It is then treated to increase its strength and make it suitable for weaving.

Like other natural fibers used for making cloth, silk is produced on farms. Silkworms are raised in controlled environments. They are given fresh mulberry leaves every couple of hours. After 4-5 weeks of almost constant consumption, the worm has grown up to 70 times its original size. It then stops eating and spins its cocoon. This takes about three days. The silk farmers can then harvest the fibers and begin to process them for use. The silk farm, therefore, is not very different in concept from a cotton farm.

Though today many items that were once made mainly of silk are made of nylon or other synthetics, silk is still a prized and treasured material.

Name: _____   **Date:** _____

1. What is the topic sentence? _____

2. In what state is Albuquerque? _____

3. What kind of balloons are in the balloon festival? _____

4. What time did the wave of balloons take off? _____

5. What word in the story means "rise up"? _____

   "come down"? _____

6. Do you think Jeannie got to ride in a balloon? _____ What makes you think so?

   _____

Balloon Fest

I got a postcard from my friend while she was on a trip to New Mexico. She said she was having lots of fun but the best thing was the balloon festival in Albuquerque. On the front was a picture of a floating balloon made to look like the face of a giant pig. Except for the tiny people hanging in the basket below, you'd never realize how big the balloon was. When she returned, Jeannie told me more about the festival.

"We got up really early—before sunrise—and headed to a large open area. There, hundreds of people were getting set for takeoff just after sunrise. The air was cold. Little fires dotted the fields, ready to inflate the balloons. I knew from science class that as air is heated it expands. The hot air inside the balloon is lighter than the outside air, causing it to rise. While riding in the balloon, the ascent or descent is controlled by adding or turning down the heat. Slowly the balloons grew from flat to fat. The balloonists were lined up in rows. At the signal, each row turned up their fires and began to rise. Row after row took to the sky in waves until there were hundreds of colorful balloons floating and bobbing above us all at once. It was the most spectacular sight I've ever seen."

Hello from...

ALBUQUERQUE

Each sentence in a paragraph has one of two roles. It is either the topic sentence (the star) or a detail (supporting cast).

Directions: *Read each sentence. Identify it as the main idea or as a detail. Write MI or D.*

(A)

_____ 1. A diamond is not only the hardest mineral known, but also one of the most valuable gems.

_____ 2. Gems are minerals that are valued for their rarity and beauty.

_____ 3. Some popular gemstones are rubies, emeralds, sapphires, and opals.

(B)

_____ 1. An octopus is a soft-bodied sea creature.

_____ 2. There are about 50 kinds of octopi, most about the size of a man's fist.

_____ 3. All octopi have eight arms, or tentacles, which are used to catch prey.

(C)

_____ 1. One way to earn money is by doing chores or services for others, such as babysitting or mowing lawns.

_____ 2. Another way is to sell things they make or have, such as setting up a drink stand or contributing to a yard sale.

_____ 3. Children have many ways to earn money for the things they want or need.

(D)

_____ 1. The Saguaro cactus is tall and thin and can grow 50 feet high!

_____ 2. Cactuses come in many shapes and sizes.

_____ 3. The barrel cactus is short and round.

Name: _____   Date: _____

Directions: *Read the sentences. First, cross out the one that does not belong with the rest. Then arrange the remaining sentences in order to make a paragraph. Begin with the sentence that gives the main idea. This will be your topic sentence. Then follow with the supporting sentences, label and color the pictures.*

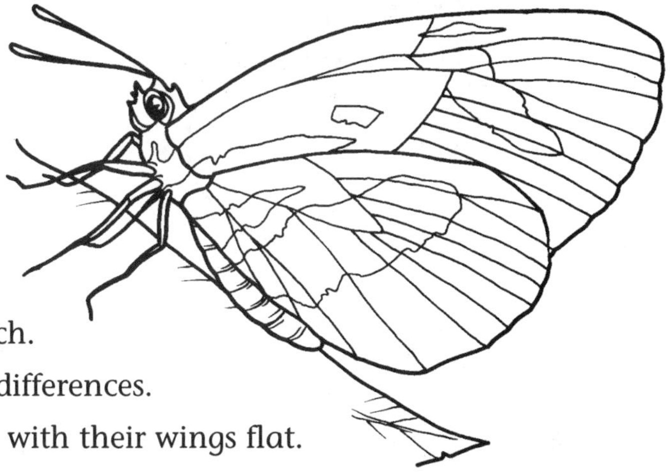

Butterflies and Moths

- Butterflies are prettier than moths.
- Can you tell butterflies and moths apart?
- It should now be easy to tell which is which.
- Both are insects, but there are noticeable differences.
- Butterflies rest with their wings up; moths with their wings flat.
- Butterflies have slender antennae; moths have feathery antennae.

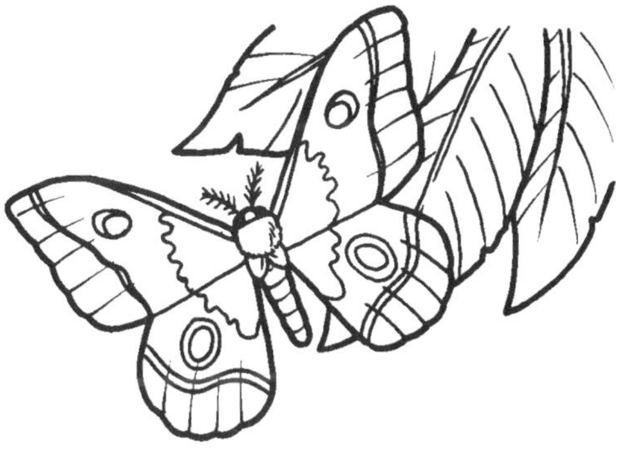

Name: ____________________ **Date:** ____________

(A)

_____ 1. Its berries give off a pleasant odor and are sweet to eat.

_____ 2. The strawberry is a small plant in the rose family.

_____ 3. Unlike true berries, the strawberry's seeds are on the outside of the fruit.

(B)

_____ 1. Charles Dickens is a revered English novelist and keen observer of life.

_____ 2. *A Christmas Carol* is perhaps his most widely known and beloved work.

_____ 3. He lived from 1812–1870.

(C)

_____ 1. It was a popular event in the Olympic Games of ancient Greece.

_____ 2. The discus throw is one of the oldest known individual sports.

_____ 3. The ancient Greeks regarded the discus throwing champion to be the greatest athlete.

(D)

_____ 1. *Sonar* stands for **SO**und **N**avigation **A**nd **R**anging.

_____ 2. It is used to measure water depth and to locate objects in the water.

_____ 3. Sonar is a method of detection using sound waves.

Name: _____   Date: _____

Sea Shells

Sea shells come in a wide variety of shapes and colors. People admire their beauty and form and enjoy looking for empty shells at the beach. They probably are not thinking about the mollusks, or soft-bodied sea creatures, that once created and inhabited most of these shells.

Four basic kinds of external sea shells exist—univalve, bivalve, tooth, and chiton. Univalves are formed in a curvy, spiral shape with a single opening at one end. Conch shells are univalves. Bivalves have two matching halves that open and close. Clam shells are examples of bivalves. Tooth shells look something like tiny, empty tusks. That is why they are sometimes also called tusk shells. Chitons (pronounced KY tuhns) are made of eight overlapping plates attached to a stretchy substance that holds them together like a rubber band.

_____

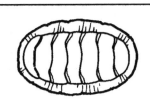
_____

_____

_____

1. What is the main idea of Paragraph 1? _____

_____

    What supports it? _____

2. Paragraph 2? _____

_____

    What supports it? _____

3. Where did many sea shells, found at the beach, originate? _____

_____

4. Mollusks such as octopus and squid have a type of shell inside their bodies. What word in the story tells you that it is only talking about shells on the outside of the body?

_____

5. Which word begins with the same sound as chiton—*children, kind,* or *city?*

_____

Here's an easy way to compare two things. In what ways are they similar, and in what ways are they different?

Directions: *Think about each pair of things. In what way can you see how they are alike? In what way are they clearly different? Write your ideas. An example is done for you.*

Example:

whale, shark

Alike: __Their bodies have similar shape for ease of swimming.__

Different: __A whale is a mammal and a shark is a fish.__

1. planet, star

   Alike: _____

   Different: _____

2. tub, sink

   Alike: _____

   Different: _____

3. watch, calendar

   Alike: _____

   Different: _____

4. photograph, painting

   Alike: _____

   Different: _____

5. lamb, calf

   Alike: _____

   Different: _____

6. orchestra, band

   Alike: _____

   Different: _____

Name: _____ **Date:** _____

People have been eating the fruit of the apple tree since ancient times. Apples remain one of the most popular fruits for eating raw and cooking. More than 2,500 different varieties are grown in the United States alone. Their colors range from deep red, to gold, to green and their tastes, from tart to sweet. They are enjoyed whole, cut up in pies and pastries, mashed into applesauce, or liquefied into juice. Their main nutritive value is as an aid to digestion. Yet apples are so highly regarded as a healthful food that many people believe that "an apple a day keeps the doctor away."

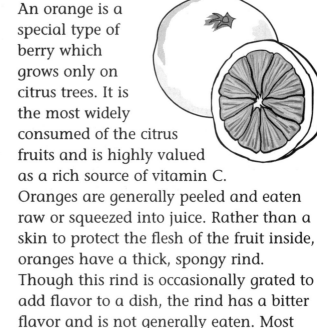

An orange is a special type of berry which grows only on citrus trees. It is the most widely consumed of the citrus fruits and is highly valued as a rich source of vitamin C. Oranges are generally peeled and eaten raw or squeezed into juice. Rather than a skin to protect the flesh of the fruit inside, oranges have a thick, spongy rind. Though this rind is occasionally grated to add flavor to a dish, the rind has a bitter flavor and is not generally eaten. Most varieties of oranges have a sweet, juicy flavor.

_____ 1. Are often enjoyed as juice

_____ 2. Edible portion is enclosed in a thick rind

_____ 3. Grow on vines

_____ 4. Are a type of citrus fruit

_____ 5. Are eaten raw

_____ 6. Are frequently served cooked

_____ 7. Keep the doctor away

_____ 8. Are often eaten whole

Name: _____   **Date:** _____

In the animal kingdom, mammals are generally grounded. The only mammal that can truly fly is the bat. The flying squirrel is named for its appearance of flying. Unlike the bat, which can move vertically, the flying squirrel can only glide from a high place to a lower one. While the bat has true wings—thin membranes of skin stretched over long slight arm bones—the flying squirrel has a furry flap of skin down each side of his body between the fully-formed front and back legs. When the flying squirrel leaps, it extends all fours, and the skin flaps form a kind of parachute, allowing it to glide gently through the air. Its tail is free and acts like a rudder for steering when moved side to side.

The flying fox is a type of bat, not a fox. Its name comes from its long slender face and snout that resemble that of a fox. It also has reddish-brown fur. About 60 varieties exist. The largest has a head and body a little longer than a foot and a wingspan of up to six feet across. It hangs upside down to sleep.

This bat eats mostly fruit and is also known as the fruit bat. That is a better name for it. It spends its days hanging in trees with other bats. At night, these bats leave their treetop roosts in droves to seek banana, pawpaw, guava, and other fruit.

Unlike other varieties of bats that use echolocation to find food, the flying fox uses its senses of sight and smell to find food. It lives in tropical regions around the world, except South America. These bats are especially common in Pacific regions.

Alike	Different
_____	_____
_____	_____
_____	_____
_____	_____
_____	_____
_____	_____
_____	_____

Name: _____   **Date:** _____

Directions: *Read the story to compare Belinda and Bianca. Then, after each statement, write TRUE or FALSE.*

A Tale of Two Cats

Once there were two cats. Belinda was Mrs. Owen's pampered pet. Bianca was on her own out and about in the neighborhood.

One day Belinda was sitting on the window sill nodding off in the sunshine. Bianca was in the alley below checking out the garbage can.

"Stop that racket," said Belinda. "Some of us are trying to take a nap."

"Well, SOME of us have to find our own food and are not given gourmet dinners by humans," answered Bianca, tossing her head in defiance. "Besides, what self-respecting cat would WANT to be owned by a human?"

Just then Bobby Jones came clumping up the alley, trying out a new shortcut home from school. He spotted Bianca.

"Oh, what a beautiful kitty," he said. "And scrounging in the garbage... Do you need a home?"

Bianca rubbed against his leg and purred. Bobby scooped her up in his arms. As he walked away with her, Bianca looked back at Belinda and pretended to yawn. She was really sticking out her tongue.

1. Belinda and Bianca are both female cats. _____

2. They both wear collars. _____

3. Mrs. Owens feeds both cats. _____

4. Bianca lives a pampered life. _____

5. Belinda and Bianca are friends. _____

6. Belinda believes she is better than Bianca. _____

7. Both cats can talk in this story. _____

8. Both cats would prefer to live with humans. _____

9. Bobby noticed both cats. _____

_____ **Date:** _____

Reading Comprehension • Saddleback Publishing, Inc. ©2002   93   3 Watson, Irvine, CA 92618•Phone (888)SDL-BACK• www.sdlback.com

It's not always easy to tell fact from opinion. Remember, a fact must be true for everyone and in all cases.

Directions: *Read the story. Then write FACT, OPINION, or DOESN'T SAY under each statement.*

In August I got to go to camp in the mountains. One of the activities was horseback riding. My horse's name was Mel, and he was the best horse in the world. It was hard to leave him when camp was over.

When I got back home I had an idea. I waited until Dad was in a good mood. Then I told him all about Mel and asked if I could have a horse.

Dad smiled. "It sounds like you had a terrific time at camp. I'm glad you enjoyed making friends with Mel. But I am afraid having a horse of your own is out of the question. Horses are very expensive to buy plus they must be boarded and fed. The family budget could not handle that kind of expense."

He paused and rubbed his chin. "What the family budget can handle is a return trip to the same camp next summer."

My eyes lit up. "Cool! I'll get to spend another week with Mel!"

1. Summer camp was a week long.

_____

2. The author of this story is a girl.

_____

3. Mel is the best horse in the world.

_____

4. Dad was glad the author had a good time at camp.

_____

5. The family has a budget.

_____

6. The family could afford to send the author to camp again.

_____

7. Dad was in a good mood when the author asked for a horse.

_____

8. The author was pleased with Dad's answer.

_____

9. The author got attached to Mel.

_____

Name: _____

Date: _____

EXAMPLE:

1. **Subject:** Your Birthday

Fact: _My birthday is in October._

Opinion: _I'd rather have my birthday be in summer._

2. **Subject:** Sports

Fact: _____

Opinion: _____

3. **Subject:** Fast-food Restaurants

Fact: _____

Opinion: _____

4. **Subject:** Teachers

Fact: _____

Opinion: _____

5. **Subject:** Tarantulas

Fact: _____

Opinion: _____

Name: _____   **Date:** _____

Take it from me, every effect has a cause. The cause is the reason, and the effect is the result.

Directions: *Write the most likely cause of each result.*

1. Kip's jeans were wet and muddy because he _____

   _____

2. Abby was late for school because she _____

   _____

3. I borrowed some money from a friend because I _____

   _____

4. We took a wrong turn because we _____

   _____

5. Donna got in trouble because she_____

   _____

6. We didn't get to see the movie this afternoon because it _____

   _____

7. Karen looked in the yellow pages because she _____

   _____

8. Jerry missed his friend Robert because he _____

   _____

- moved last month.
- went to visit him.
- was making noise in the library.
- forgot my lunch money.
- was sold out.

- didn't have a map.
- was raining.
- overslept this morning.
- rode his bike through some puddles.
- needed the number of Pizza King.

Name: _____   **Date:** _____

affect: to cause; influence	**effect**: the result of an action

1. The weather will _____ our picnic plans.

2. What _____ did the medicine have on your cold?

3. The fire had a devastating _____ on the forest.

4. A cavity can be the _____ of eating too much sugar.

5. My pleading did not _____ Dad's decision.

6. Did your apology have any _____?

7. Tides are the _____ of the moon's gravity on the oceans.

8. Incomplete homework will _____ your final grade.

9. Not having breakfast can _____ your work at school.

10. Dry ice gave the stage an eerie _____.

11. I will not let the noise _____ my concentration.

12. How did the news about Mrs. Chan _____ you?

13. Laundering had no _____ on the stain.

14. The heat may _____ the players on the field.

15. Dampness will _____ the durability of cardboard.

16. Your get-well card had a cheery _____.

17. What _____ do people have on the environment?

18. This game will _____ the standings in the playoffs.

Name: _____ **Date:** _____

Creating a mental picture of a character you meet makes the character come alive.

Directions: *Read the story. Write your conclusions on the lines below.*

The only thing Lisa loved more than horses was competing in shows. She and Mr. K had won several ribbons. A big show was coming up on Saturday, but during their workout Wednesday, Lisa's dad noticed that Mr. K was favoring his back right foot a bit. Henri told Lisa that he wanted the vet to see him and to clear him for competition. The vet lived just over the hill, so Henri called her, and she came right over.

After looking at Mr. K the vet let out a sigh. "I'm afraid Mr. K cannot be in any shows for awhile. He needs at least two weeks' rest before he can compete again."

Lisa didn't want to hear any of that. While putting Mr. K back into his stall, Lisa murmured to herself about how unfair it was. When she came in the house for dinner, she slammed the door.

"Whoa, young lady," said Henri. Lisa folded her arms and scowled.

Henri put his arm around her. "I know you are disappointed, but think about Mr. K. Isn't his well-being more important than a show?"

One corner of her mouth turned up a little. Then the other. "I'm sorry. You're right. I love

1. Who is Mr. K? _____ Henri? _____

2. What kind of a person is Henri? _____

_____

3. Why did Lisa slam the door? _____

4. Was the vet a man or woman? _____

5. Do you think Lisa will be punished for her behavior and attitude? _____

   Why or why not? _____

6. Is Lisa's family well-off or not? _____ What makes you think so?

_____

Name: _____   **Date:** _____

Before the boxes were even unpacked Sam went all over the house exploring. He found little hidden closets, cubby holes, and to his delight, an attic! It was a bit dusty and nearly empty, but over in the corner was a box. Sam went right to it and looked inside. At first he frowned—a crummy old doll—but wait, under it was a pack of letters tied in red ribbon. He looked at the envelopes. They were addressed to an Ellie Rivers at this house.

Later, he asked his parents if they could find out if an Ellie Rivers lived at this house before they did, and he told them about the doll. Mrs. Larson said that perhaps the real estate agent would know.

Sure enough, the Rivers family, who had lived in the house before, did have a young girl. The agent gave Sam the new address and he immediately wrote to them asking if Ellie would write him back.

About a week later a letter came for Sam. It was from Kathy Rivers. She wondered how Sam had known her Grandma Ellie, who used to live with them, but was now in a retirement community about five miles from the Larsons. "Ah ha" thought Sam, and he showed Mom the letter and told her his plan.

On Saturday, the Larsons drove to the retirement community. Ellie Rivers looked puzzled when they came into her room, but soon her face lit up. "Oh my goodness!" she beamed, "It's Molly! I thought I had lost her years ago."

1. Which of the following terms best describes Sam's character: thoughtful, self-absorbed, disinterested, solitary, or hesitant? _____

2. Why didn't Ellie Rivers write back to Sam? _____
   _____

3. How did Sam's parents react to his strange request? _____
   _____

4. What action did Sam take that showed he was curious? _____
   _____

5. Why do you think Sam went to all the trouble he did to find Ellie Rivers? _____
   _____

6. At the end of the story, what do you think Ellie thought about Sam as a person? _____
   _____

Name: _____ **Date:** _____

Directions: *Read the questions below. Keep them in mind as you read the tale. Then go back and answer them.*

It is natural for us, as humans, to think about things from a "human" point of view. Take time, for example. Although time passes at the same rate for all living things, the lifespan of any particular species varies greatly. To us, a year is perhaps $\frac{1}{70}$ of a lifetime. To an animal that lives about 2 years, it is $\frac{1}{2}$ of its life.

In general, large animals have longer lifespans that small ones. Does this mean that small animals live "faster" than large ones? The rate of living, or metabolism, can be measured by counting the number of times the heart beats and number of breaths that are taken in a minute. A small shrew's heart may beat 800 times a minute, and it may take about 200 breaths. During the same minute, an elephant's heart ticks 25 times, and it takes just 6 breaths. The shrew's metabolism is going about 30 times faster than the elephant's—thirty "shrew" days is equivalent to one "elephant" day.

We cannot know if our mammal friends perceive the passage of time differently than we do, but some scientists say that all mammals have about 200 million breaths and 1000 million heartbeats in them. What about us? According to that formula, for our size, we should last about 30 years. In fact, before modern medicine and other developments that have lengthened our lifespan, we did little better than that.

1. Does an elephant live about 30 times longer than a small shrew? _____

2. Does time pass more quickly for small mammals than large ones? _____

3. From whose point of view do you learn this information? _____

4. What factor, other than metabolism, may affect the actual length of life of any animal?

   _____

5. Why might today's humans generally outlive their projected metabolic lifespan?

   _____

6. After reading this article what is your perspective on the passage of time? _____

   _____

Name: _____   **Date:** _____

My home, the city of Los Angeles, California, is home to not only a prodigious population, but also a large number of icons instantly recognized around the world.

Besides Hollywood, the Rose Parade, and the infamous smog and traffic, Los Angeles has one of the busiest airports in the world. About 200,000 passengers pass through Los Angeles International Airport (LAX) each day! It is the second busiest cargo airport in the world, carrying some 2.1 million tons a year. By 2010 it is estimated that LAX will handle double that amount of cargo and 94 million passengers annually.

With all of this traffic, it is no wonder that LAX is a well-known landmark. Standing in its center is a huge spaceship-looking structure. Four legs support a giant rotating disk. When first seen, many people assume that it is the control tower. But it is a restaurant, which, while you dine, gives you a ride and a 360° view!

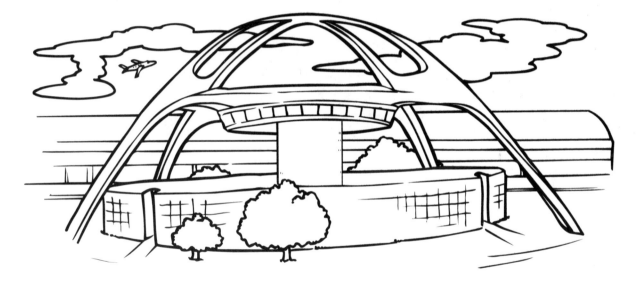

1. From whose perspective is the story written? _____

2. How does the author appears to feel about the city of Los Angeles? _____

   the airport? _____

3. How might someone from a small Midwestern town feel upon arriving at LAX? _____

   _____

4. Imagine that you were coming to Los Angeles for the first time. Would this story make you feel excited, nervous, overwhelmed, curious, or something else? _____

   _____

   Why? _____

Name: _____   **Date:** _____

Directions: Using only the information you can conclude from this scene of young children, decide if the statement is true, false, or can't be determined.

1. The weather outdoors this day is comfortable.

   O true   O false   O can't be determined

2. The dog belongs to the boy.

   O true   O false   O can't be determined

3. The children are all the same age.

   O true   O false   O can't be determined

4. The girls are paying attention to the boy.

   O true   O false   O can't be determined

5. The children are sitting on a sidewalk.

   O true   O false   O can't be determined

6. They are eating lunch together.

   O true   O false   O can't be determined

Name: _____   **Date:** _____

Not that it would ever need to, but the South American electric eel can discharge enough electricity to stun a horse—over 600 volts worth. That's quite a shocker!

Though not as dramatic, other fish have electrical shock abilities, too. The torpedo ray gives off an average of 60 volts, but some species can generate a healthy 200 volts—quite useful and effective on both their predators and their prey.

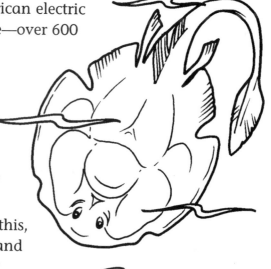

Other animals may not have built-in "death rays," but all animals use electricity in some way. Don't think you have electric power? As you are reading this, electrical impulses are hard at work in your brain and nerves sending and receiving messages throughout your body.

1. Based on this story, what can you conclude that all animals have in common?

   _____

2. If not horses, what do you think the electric eel uses its tremendous shock for?

   _____

3. Does the torpedo ray have any natural enemies? _____ How do you know?

   _____

4. What are two different possible meanings of "shocking" in this story?

   _____

5. What does "healthy" mean in the second paragraph? _____

6. Do you think the South American electric eel has the most powerful shock ability of all animals? _____ Why or why not? _____

   _____

1. It blew over in the wind.

   It can't be

   O castle.
   O a lawn chair.
   O a sign.

2. It pecked at the seeds scattered on the ground.

   It can't be

   O a pelican.
   O a chicken.
   O a robin.

3. I see something shiny on the ground.

   It can't be

   O a star.
   O an earring.
   O a silver coin.

4. A one-foot square box came in the mail.

   It can't be

   O a stuffed animal.
   O a bike.
   O some books.

5. Something just came in for a landing in the open field.

   It can't be

   O a plane.
   O an eagle.
   O an army.

6. Mr. Robins popped the sweet treat into the oven.

   It can't be

   O a pie.
   O a roast.
   O a cake.

7. Danielle opened it and smiled.

   It can't be

   O the door.
   O a letter.
   O the phone.

8. I lost it. It must have fallen out of my pocket on the way home.

   It can't be

   O a jacket.
   O a key.
   O a dollar.

9. Bill looked in his dresser drawer and found something unexpected.

   It can't be

   O his library book.
   O his missing pet snake.
   O his little sister.

Reading Comprehension • Saddleback Publishing, Inc. ©2002   104   3 Watson, Irvine, CA 92618•Phone (888)SDL-BACK•www.sdlback.com

1. Haley bought a mouse for her pet. What is her pet?

   ___ a cat   ___ a snake   ____ a dog

2. David saved up his allowance for nine weeks. He had enough to get

   ___ a college education   ____ a new bike   ____ a video game

3. Dario ran home from school with the news. It was that

   ___ he had straight A's   ____ his school was closed   ____ he broke his leg

4. Late last night Karen heard a noise outside her window. It was a

   ___ tree struck by lightning   ____ UFO landing   ____ raccoon in the trash

5. Renee found a stray in the alley. It was

   ___ a kitten with no tail   ____ a cat with a cut on its ear   ____ a baby lion

6. The doctor treated Christopher for an allergic reaction to a

   ___ scorpion bite   ____ wolf attack   ____ bee sting

7. After his haircut, Eddie looked in the mirror and was surprised because

   ___ he was bald   ____ he looked great   ____ his hair looked darker

8. Arthur was thrilled and could not wait to get home to tell his parents about the soccer game. He was thrilled because

   ___ he sat on the sidelines throughout the game   ____ he scored the winning goal

   ____ his coach praised his efforts on the field

Name: _____   **Date:** _____

Try this! When you read for information, make a mental file of facts you want to remember.

Directions: *Below are some math problems that can't be solved because an important piece of information is missing. Read carefully, then write what else you would need to know to be able to solve the problem. An example is done for you.*

Example: Mr. Hall ordered from Mr. May's factory 120 cans of soup for his market. Mr. May can ship twenty 16-oz. cans or fifteen 24-oz. cans per box. How many boxes will he need to ship Mr. Hall's order?

What else do you need to know to solve the problem?

what size cans Mr. Hall ordered

1.
Jack and Joe were in a 100-meter relay race. Jack ran the first half and Joe the second. Their total speed was 18.2 seconds. Who ran the 50 meters faster?

What else do you need to know to solve the problem?

_____

_____

2.
A submarine could travel at 32 km per hour. If it makes only two short stops per week, how far can it travel in two weeks?

What else do you need to know to solve the problem?

_____

_____

3.
Celia needed four batteries for a toy. She saw packs of 6 AA batteries and packs of 8 AAA batteries for the same price. Which should she buy?

What else do you need to know to solve the problem?

_____

_____

4.
At the school picnic, 230 hotdogs and 175 hamburgers were sold. Drinks were sold separately. A total of 75% of all the people at the picnic ordered a lemonade. How many lemonades were sold?

What else do you need to know to solve the problem?

_____

_____

Name: _____   **Date:** _____

A Wolf's "Tail"

When we are relaxed, fearful, upset or angry, we let others know our feelings by simply saying them in words. Wolves use their tails to convey these feelings.

If the tail is relaxed and hanging loosely, the wolf is relaxed and "hanging loose." If he is holding his tail down with the fur flattened and the tip upturned, he is letting others know that he is not a threat. When the wolf is afraid, however, the tail will curve down under his body with the tip toward his stomach.

What signals indicate anger or aggression? If the tail is held high and straight, with fur fluffed, the wolf is indicating "back off." If the tail is held straight out behind him, however, he is signaling that he is ready to attack.

You may have observed dogs' tails in these positions. Dogs, close relatives of the wolf, often use the same signals.

1. Wolves and dogs use their tails to convey feelings.

2. Cats also convey feelings with the position of their tails.

3. A wolf is most dangerous when his tail is held up high.

_____

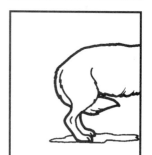

4. Wolves also communicate through howls and barks.

_____

5. If a wolf was afraid, his tail would be curved under him.

_____

Name: _____   **Date:** _____

Woodpeckers

Woodpeckers are known for the unmistakable sound of their mating call—the hammering of their bill against a tree or other surface.

Woodpeckers use their strong, chisel-like bills to bore holes in the trunks of trees. It is here that they find the juicy insects that compose the mainstay of their diet. A woodpecker's body is designed to help it cling to the tree's trunk. Its feet have four toes—two pointing forward, and two backward—giving it a good grip. Also its tail has stiff feathers that help balance and support its body as it climbs or hangs on to the tree. Woodpeckers' tongues are long, usually have thorny barbed tips, and are coated with a sticky saliva. The bird thrusts its tongue into the hole, spears the insect, then pulls it out. The sticky saliva also helps them gather smaller insects such as ants.

Many varieties of woodpeckers exist. Some are common and others are rare. Their colors and features differ. For example, some woodpeckers have smooth feathers; others have a more downy look. Some have crests; some do not.

_____ 1. Woodpeckers are a type of bird.

_____ 2. A woodpecker's diet may include berries, fruits, and nuts.

_____ 3. Woodpeckers make an unmistakable sound.

_____ 4. A woodpecker can bore a hole in a tree.

_____ 5. Some woodpeckers have crests.

_____ 6. A cartoon character was based on the redheaded woodpecker.

_____ 7. Woodpeckers live on all continents except Australia and Antarctica.

_____ 8. Some insects live inside tree trunks.

_____ 9. Young woodpeckers hatch without any feathers.

Name: _____   **Date:** _____

Directions: *Read the story. Then, follow the directions for Part I and Part II.*

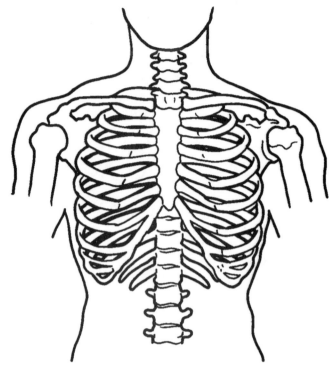

Ribs

Most vertebrates, or animals with backbones, have ribs. Ribs are the sets of bones that encase the soft organs of the chest, including the heart and lungs. The number of ribs vary with the type of animal. Some whales, for example, have nine pairs of ribs, while a two-toed sloth has twenty-four pairs. Humans have twelve pairs of ribs.

In humans, all twelve ribs on each side of the body are connected to the backbone, or spine. The upper seven pair are also connected to the sternum, or breastbone, in the front of the body. These are called true ribs. The five lower pairs are called false ribs. The upper three sets of these are attached with cartilage. The bottom two sets are called floating ribs because they are only attached to the spine and "float" unattached in the front.

Part I. Fill in the bubble of the correct answer.

1. How many rib bones does a human have?
   - O 12
   - O 24

2. What is another name for sternum?
   - O vertebrate
   - O breastbone

3. True or False? The larger the animal the more ribs it will have.
   - O True
   - O False

4. To what are floating ribs attached?
   - O spine
   - O nothing

5. What are the five lower pairs of ribs called?
   - O true ribs
   - O false ribs

6. Which of the following would not have ribs?
   - O vertebrate
   - O invertebrate

7. Which ribs are attached with cartilage?
   - O the upper 3 sets of false ribs
   - O the lower 2 sets of false ribs

Part II. On the diagram, color true ribs blue, floating ribs red, and the remaining false ribs green.

Name: _____   **Date:** _____

Directions: *Read the story. Then answer the questions below.*

California Gold

About 150 years ago, gold was discovered in California, and a rush to move there began. It seems that people have been coming ever since.

I live in California—the Golden State—and for me the gold is not shiny nuggets but sunshine. Here on the southern California coast, we have one of the most pleasant climates in the world. We have few days that are uncomfortably hot or cold and even fewer days that are rainy or gloomy.

Some people say that not having drastic seasons would be boring. They would miss the crisp air of fall, the sweltering dog days of summer, and maybe, especially, the first fresh snow of winter. Those things are nice, but I'll keep the "boring" warm sunshine day in and day out.

Besides, it's not as if we don't ever have changes in the weather. During the winter months of December through February, while much of the rest of the United States is buried in snow and ice or battling the freezing cold, I also have to adjust to colder temperatures—sometimes I have to wear a jacket!

1. Which word best describes the author's tone in this story?

   O swaggering   O apologetic   O wistful

2. Which best describes the author's intent for the meaning of the title?

   O the Gold Rush of 1849   O the Golden State   O the sunshine

3. Is this passage fact, opinion, or a mixture of both?

   O fact   O opinion   O mixture

4. Evaluate: *In Southern California it is cooler in winter than in other months.*

   O true   O false   O story doesn't say

5. Which best states the main idea of the passage?

   O California is named the Golden State because of the Gold Rush.

   O The weather in southern California is mild and some people like it.

   O Living without drastic changes in seasons can be boring.

Name: _____   **Date:** _____

1. From where did the author emigrate to America? _____

2. How does the author feel about bonsai? _____

3. What main ideas does the author want you to know about bonsai? _____

_____

4. According to the author, what are the hallmarks of Japanese art and culture? _____

_____

5. Why do you think the author cannot have a bonsai garden here in America? _____

_____

Bonsai Trees

My name is Meiko. When my family moved to the United States, we brought many of our customs with us. Among my favorites is the art of bonsai. Harmony, beauty, simplicity, and balance are hallmarks of Japanese art and culture. Among other things, the Japanese are known for their simple but thoughtfully designed gardens. Each rock, pool, temple, or gateway is positioned where it can best be admired and where it complements other elements of the garden arrangement.

Bonsai, another form of garden, is the Japanese art of producing miniature, but fully formed, trees. This is done by precise clipping of branches and roots, and carefully regulating the water supply. Bonsai tree arrangements are so small that they can be placed within a home instead of outside it.

The art of bonsai originated in China but became popular in Japan around 1500. Some bonsai trees are very old and have been passed from one generation to another. For this reason bonsai trees are considered a symbol of immortality in the Japanese culture.

I brought with me to America a small bonsai tree. But, alas, we cannot have a whole garden.

Name: _____   **Date:** _____

Ever wonder how the wolf would have told the story of Little Red Riding Hood? Each character has his or her own twist on things. This is called point of view.

Directions: *As you read this story, think about it from each character's point of view—Noreen's, the dove's, and Gus's. Then you'll be ready to answer the questions.*

One of Great Aunt Noreen's favorite things to do is to sit out on the porch in her wicker rocker and observe life.

One day, Noreen was watching Gus, the neighborhood stray cat, run across the lawn

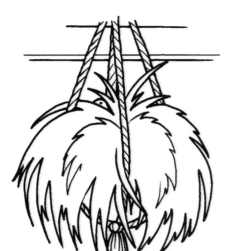

and scamper up and down a tree. Noreen admired the spunk in the little guy.

Just then she heard a rustling above and behind her left ear—right where her fern plant hung low from the porch eaves. Noreen raised herself up from the cushion just high enough to see that a dove was sitting on a nest in her hanging plant. Though no more than three feet away, the bird didn't budge.

Noreen smiled, but as she sat back down, her smile faded to dismay. The mother dove need not be afraid to have her family around Noreen, but what about having her family around Gus?

1. Describe Gus from Noreen's point of view. _____
   _____

2. Describe Noreen from Gus's point of view. _____
   _____

3. From the dove's point of view, why did she choose the fern plant to nest in? _____
   _____

4. Why do you think the dove did not budge when Noreen spotted her? _____
   _____

5. How did Noreen's view of Gus change after she discovered the dove? _____
   _____

Name: _____   **Date:** _____

A Little Enticement

The old man loaded up the donkey with his wares. But instead of moving, the donkey just sat. When he yanked on his rope, the donkey brayed. Frustrated, the man sat down next to his donkey with his face buried in his hands. Just as he was considering his predicament, the donkey rose and began to walk. Bewildered, the man caught up with him. Soon he saw what made the old donkey move. Up ahead on the path was another man heading to market—with a cart full of fresh vegetables.

	Man	Donkey
1. Two words to describe his feeling:		
2. What his motivation is:		
3. Something he would be thinking:		
4. Something he would say to the other:		

Explain why the author chose the title "A Little Enticement." _____

_____

Name: _____   **Date:** _____

Reading Comprehension • Saddleback Publishing, Inc. ©2002   113   3 Watson, Irvine, CA 92618 • Phone (888) SDL-BACK • www.sdlback.com

An author gets you ready to read by setting the stage—telling you where and when the story takes place.

1. Captain Newton woke up in a small barren room with a single way out, but when he tried it, he was stopped by a force field. "I can cut through it with my laser," thought the captain, but when he reached for it, it was gone. Luckily the Delaxians had not removed his portable communicator...

The setting is in the _____

I concluded this from _____

_____

_____

2. On Friday the Burks got into their van and headed for the video store. The store was having a promotion. If your rental receipt had a red star, you won a coupon good for five free movie rentals. The children waited eagerly as the clerk rung up their selection. And, there it was, plain as day—a big red star on the receipt!

The setting is in the _____

I concluded this from _____

_____

_____

3. Steven sat on the porch with his dad, staring at the clear night sky. The moon was full and bright. Just a few days ago, they heard on the news that John Glenn had become the first American to orbit the Earth in a spacecraft. Steven looked at the moon and said, "Do you think people will ever reach as far as the moon, Dad?"

The setting is in the _____

I concluded this from _____

_____

_____

4. Susan put on her best dress and bonnet. Today her family would join many others on a wagon train west. She'd heard stories, of course, about exciting things and scary things other settlers had encountered. She petted Old Jed's nose. "You'll be all right," she said aloud, more to reassure herself than the horse.

The setting is in the _____

I concluded this from _____

_____

_____

Name: _____   **Date:** _____

Barry is quite an adventurer—in his dreams! Below Barry is telling you a little about some of his dreams, but in each he left out the setting. Fill it in from the choices below.

1. We were

_____

_____

when I spotted a bear coming right toward us.

2. I was the bravest knight

_____

_____

and easily won the joust.

3. I was on safari

_____

_____

following a group of kangaroos.

4. Despite the bitter wind and cold, I lead the climber to

_____

_____.

5. While living

_____

_____,

I was the first human to be adopted by gorillas.

- in King Arthur's court
- in the outback of Australia
- camping in the woods
- in the heart of Africa
- the top of Mt. Everest

Name: _____   **Date:** _____

Directions: Test your skill at "reading between the lines." Hidden in each description below is a clue to the time frame in which it is happening. Hint: Even if you don't know for sure, you can use the clue to eliminate the other choices. Circle your choice, then explain why. The first one is done for you.

Paul and Samuel were concerned when they heard the news on the radio. War seemed imminent.

The time frame is the period of   **Revolutionary War**   **Civil War**   (**Gulf War**)

because ___radio had not been invented at the time of the other two___.

1. He looked through his crude telescope and was the first to see the four largest moons of Jupiter and the rings of Saturn.

   The time frame is   **1000 B.C.**   **1610 A.D.**   **1963 A.D.**

   because _____.

2. The hunter proudly communicated to his tribe that he had killed a wooly mammoth and there would be food enough for all.

   The time frame is   **prehistoric**   **height of Roman Empire**   **modern times**

   because _____.

3. Laden in heavy suits, the men and women trained for long periods in space.

   The time frame is   **1999 A.D.**   **1888 A.D.**   **1160 A.D.**

   because _____.

4. When the ship arrived, the Native Americans were bewildered. They had never seen a European before.

   The time frame is   **400 B.C.**   **1492 A.D.**   **1776 A.D.**

   because _____.

Name: _____   **Date:** _____

Dear Diary,
I hate Sundays. There is football on all day and my whole family watches except me. Wednesday is Mom's birthday, so I think I'll go make her a card.

Dear Diary,
I got an A on my social studies test yesterday—duh. Also, Jenny invited me to a party Saturday at the skating rink. That's only four days away—cool. Tonight I made a cake from scratch for Mom's birthday tomorrow.

Dear Diary,
Get this—DAD cooked dinner last night for Mom's birthday. He made spaghetti and was pretending to sing in Italian. It wasn't bad, but if he wanted Italian, ordering pizza would have been easier, especially because I had to clean up. Gotta go. Math quiz tomorrow.

Dear Diary,
Last night I went to the mall to get Jenny something for her party today. I got her a diary! What do you think?

EVENTS:

- Mom's birthday
- made a cake
- went to the mall
- Dad cooked
- made a card
- got invited to party
- Jenny's party
- math quiz
- got an A on test

SUN.	MON.	TUES.	WED.	THURS.	FRI.	SAT.
17	18	19	20	21	22	23

Reading Comprehension • Saddleback Publishing, Inc. ©2002   117   3 Watson, Irvine, CA 92618•Phone (888)SDL-BACK•www.sdlback.com

Compare the plot of the classic fable "The Tortoise and the Hare" to a fiction story you have recently read or remember well. Complete the table for your story choice.

Directions: Compare the plot of the classic fable *The Tortoise and the Hare* to a fiction story you have recently read or remember well. Complete the table for your story choice.

	Story #1	Story #2
Story Title	The Tortoise and the Hare	
Main Characters	Tortoise Hare	
Problem or Conflict	Each expects to win the race	
Key Events	• Hare thinks he has time for a nap. • While Hare naps, Tortoise passes him. • Tortoise plods across the finish line.	
Outcome	Tortoise wins the race.	

Reading Comprehension • Saddleback Publishing, Inc. ©2002   118   3 Watson, Irvine, CA 92618•Phone (888)SDL-BACK•www.sdlback.com

Just Another Day

Mary Ann woke up in a good mood. Today was a special day for her. Usually on this day, she'd find a card next to her breakfast plate. There would be a balloon tied to her chair. Later, after dinner there would be cake and presents from her family.

When Mary Ann went down to breakfast, all that was next to her plate was a napkin and silverware. Her chair looked the same as always. No one said anything out of the ordinary.

At school, Mary Ann's teacher asked why she looked so sad. She said she didn't feel well, which was true in a way.

At 3:00 Mary Ann walked slowly home from school. She paused at the door and sighed. When she stepped inside her eyes lit up. The room was decorated top to bottom and filled with balloons.

"Surprise!" shouted her Mom, Dad, Grandma, and big brother. Even baby Emily made a happy sound.

1. What is the main idea of this story?

   O A girl gets a birthday surprise.   O Mary Ann is disappointed.   O A family forgets a special birthday.

2. Why did Mary Ann wake up in a good mood?

   O It was Christmas.   O It was her birthday.   O It was Saturday.

3. When did Mary Ann's family usually have cake and presents?

   O at breakfast   O at school   O in the evening

4. When Mary Ann said she didn't feel well, what probably was hurting?

   O her feelings   O her stomach   O her feet

5. Of the children in Mary Ann's family, Mary Ann is the

   O oldest child   O youngest child   O middle child

6. When Mary Ann was walking home from school, she probably felt

   O disappointed   O angry   O worried

Name: _____   **Date:** _____

You have moods—silly, serious, mysterious, or quiet. Stories have moods, too—created by subject, word use, and pictures.

Directions: *Below are some made-up book titles. Based on the titles, what two words do you think would describe the mood of the story? Write them on the book's cover. Use words from the list or add your own*

THE DUDLEYS GO TO MARS	**WATSON FINDS THE FINAL CLUE**	**DIVING FOR LOST TREASURE**
HAUNTED CASTLE	**THE SECRET CAVE**	**MR. MARSH'S MAGNIFICENT MACHINE**
TROUBLE WITH TWINS	**LIVING IN SILENCE:** A Deaf Person's Diary	**IF YOU HAD TRAVELED IN A COVERED WAGON**

Mood Words

lighthearted
mysterious
silly
scary
serious
adventurous
creepy
puzzling
dark
strange
exciting
informative
entertaining
whimsical
eerie
suspenseful
calm
mischievous
light
historical
educational
humorous

Name: _____

Date: _____

Directions: *The two poems below are about summer days. As you read them, think about moods they create. Then answer the questions below.*

Another summer day is here
And as soon as it is new
My mind fills up with a long list
Of things that I could do.

I could take a nap or read a book
Beneath the willow tree,
Or get my silly brother
To take a swim with me.

I could fill a pitcher to the top
With lemonade so sweet,
Or just take off my shoes and socks
And walk barefoot in the creek.

The willow's branches
Hanging heavy
Sagging in the summer sun.

The bright flower's petals
Drooping listless
Thirsty in the summer heat.

The thoughts in my head
Drifting forward
Longing for summer's end.

1. Is the setting the same or different in the two poems? _____

2. Do the writers feel the same or different about summer days? _____

3. What is the mood created in the first poem? _____

4. Identify at least four words that clearly set the tone of the first poem: _____

_____

5. What is the mood created in the second poem? _____

6. Identify at least four words that clearly set the tone of the second poem: _____

_____

7. What specific thing is mentioned in both poems? _____

Here's how to cook up a summary. Boil the information down to just the main ideas.

Directions: *Read the story. Then, write TRUE or FALSE under each statement. Finally, write the main idea of this story. Use the back of this page as needed.*

1. The Celts primarily inhabited southern Europe.

   _____

2. The Celts were a single tribe of people.

   _____

3. They inhabited Europe about two thousand years ago.

   _____

4. The Celts lived in caves.

   _____

5. They made tools and weapons out of metal.

   _____

6. None of their crafts survive to this day.

   _____

7. Celtic metal crafts are distinguished by decorative knotwork and animal designs.

   _____

Main Idea: _____

_____

_____

The Celts (pronounced Kelts) were a network of tribes that inhabited much of western Europe about two thousand years ago. Although they shared a similar way of life, each tribe was different. Most Celtic tribes lived in small villages or in huts.

The Celts are known for being proud, fierce, artistic, and learned people. They were skilled farmers, warriors, poets, and metalworkers. A large portion of their tools and weapons were made of metals such as iron, bronze, copper, gold, and silver. Many of their beautiful metal craftworks survive to this day. They can be distinguished as Celtic by the intricate and decorative knotwork and stylized animals etched into the metal.

Name: _____   **Date:** _____

It was the last week of school. The principal wanted to recognize students who had made outstanding achievements that year. She had awards made up and called an assembly to give them out.

No one knew who would be getting an award. The students sat nervously as Mrs. Collings stepped up to the microphone.

"Our first award is for excellence in science. It goes to Derek Farland for his project on heredity."

As Derek came up to accept the award, his classmates applauded.

Mrs. Collings continued to call the names of deserving students for outstanding reading, math, sports, school spirit, and more. As each person was recognized, the students cheered.

Finally, the last award was announced. "For perfect attendance, the honor goes to Tina Meller, who has not been absent once the whole year."

The room fell silent. Then there was a muffle of laughter. Tim Liddy stood up and said with a smile, "Tina is home sick today."

1. Which sentence states the main point of the story?
   - O Derek Linden got the science award.
   - O Tina Meller was absent for the perfect attendance award.
   - O The principal recognized students for outstanding achievements.

2. Which would be the best title?
   - O Imperfect Timing
   - O Outstanding Achievements
   - O The Last Week at School

3. What was the author's purpose?
   - O to inform the reader
   - O to persuade the reader
   - O to entertain the reader

4. The author used a type of humor called *irony*. Based on the story, which of these best describes irony?
   - O a surprise turn in a direction opposite of what is expected
   - O to make a joke about or poke fun at something
   - O to use the wrong words on purpose so the result sounds funny

5. Do you think Tina should still get the award? _____ Why or why not?

_____

Name: _____   **Date:** _____

Directions: *Read the story. Think about each question, then answer YES or NO.*

1. A river can carve out rock.

   _____

2. The Colorado River is an example of an "old" river.

   _____

3. "Old" rivers do not cause erosion.

   _____

4. The Mississippi River drains into the Gulf of Mexico.

   _____

5. The Colorado River has created a broad, flat valley.

   _____

6. It takes many years for a young turbulent river to reduce a boulder to mud.

   _____

7. The Mississippi River can flood in the spring.

   _____

8. The Colorado and Mississippi Rivers are about the same age.

   _____

Rivers—Young and Old

Among the forces that sculpt the landscape of the earth, rivers and streams do more to shape the land than all others combined.

Running water from melting snow and ice scrapes the exposed rocks of mountains. Loose bits of stone dig at the sides and create steep-walled canyons. Though it takes a long time to carve a canyon, a young, turbulent river can break apart a six-foot boulder and reduce it to mud in just a few short years. The Colorado River is such a force.

More mature rivers create broad, flat valleys. But even an "old" river like the Mississippi can be a formidable force of erosion. During a spring flood, the Mississippi carries about 10 million tons of earth from North America to the Gulf of Mexico each day!

Name: _____   **Date:** _____

Directions: *Sometimes when a decision has to be made, people do not all agree. Opinions are gathered to consider. In each situation below, imagine that you have been asked for your input. Give your opinion and reasons for it. Write a persuasive argument for your point of view.*

1. Several students in your class want to be kindergarten monitors. Only two can be selected for the job. How do you think they should be chosen? Why?

_____

_____

_____

_____

2. Your parents announce that they have decided to set aside the second Friday of each month as "Family Night," on which everyone in the family will go out to dinner together. How do you think it should be decided where the family will eat? Why?

_____

_____

_____

_____

_____

3. A notice is sent out that tryouts for the soccer team will be at noon on Saturday. Your best friend really wants to be on the team but already said she would come to your party. What do you think she should do? Why?

_____

_____

_____

_____

Name: _____   **Date:** _____

Directions: In each blank, fill in the sentence that makes the most sense in the story.

Josh was crazy about dolphins. His room was filled with them—stuffed ones, ceramic ones, glass ones, and wax ones. _____

_____

_____. Josh dreamed of having a real dolphin of his own but knew, of course, that could never be. He'd never even seen a real dolphin. Then he got an idea. Dad said that if his grades continued to be good, he could do something special for his birthday this summer. It was a long shot, but he did it. _____

_____.

Josh was stunned when Dad agreed. They made plans to go in June.

When the big day arrived, Josh was beside himself. _____

_____

_____. Then, in the middle of the show, the trainer announced that it was Josh's birthday, and a certain dolphin wanted to give him a kiss. Josh went to the tank and Dolly popped up and clicked at him, then rubbed her snout against his cheek. Josh was still beaming when he got back to his seat. He leaned over to Dad. _____

_____

Dad just smiled and winked.

- He also had some stuffed whales, but he didn't like them as much.
- Their pictures were on the walls and books about them were on the shelves.
- He asked Dad if they could go to Sea World and see real dolphins.
- He decided to ask for a real dolphin.
- "How did they know...?" he asked.
- Sure enough, he got to see real dolphins playing and performing.
- "That was Dolly," he said.

Name: _____   **Date:** _____

- Once, Uncle Cal built a shed out back for dad.

- Then he made a super doghouse for our dog, Sport.

- When it comes to building things, my Uncle Cal really knows what he's doing.

- Plus, when Grandma wanted a new trellis for her roses, Uncle Cal designed and built one by hand.

- Uncle Cal is my mom's younger brother.

- And he does all this on weekends, when he's not at his job as a carpenter!

_____

_____

_____

_____

_____

_____

_____

_____

_____

_____

_____

_____

_____

To be a good detective, you have to know what facts are important and not important to the case you're solving! So, ask yourself questions as you read.

Directions: Read the questions below. Keep them in mind as you read the story. Then go back and answer them.

1. Where does the story take place? _____

2. What was the purpose of the trip? _____

3. What does unaccompanied mean? _____

4. How can you tell Joshua was nervous? _____

5. Why do you think Joshua saluted instead of just waving? _____

_____

6. How long would Joshua be gone? _____

7. Why do you think the attendant put a special sticker on Joshua's jacket? _____

_____

It was a short flight, and only for the weekend, but Joshua had mixed feelings. On one hand he was excited to being going to visit his dad. On the other hand, he had never flown alone before.

Joshua fidgeted in his seat. Mom patted him on the arm reassuredly. Then the announcement came over the waiting area. "We are now ready to board people with special needs and unaccompanied children."

"I guess this is it," he mumbled. He picked up his bag and went toward the gate.

"Call me as soon as you get there," said Mom and gave Joshua a hug.

Joshua handed the attendant his ticket, and she placed a special sticker on his jacket shaped like wings that said "Junior VIP." Joshua felt a little silly but was kind of glad he was given special attention. He smiled, gave his Mom a salute, and walked down the jetway.

Name: _____   Date: _____

Reading Comprehension • Saddleback Publishing, Inc. ©2002   128   3 Watson, Irvine, CA 92618•Phone (888)SDL-BACK•www.sdlback.cor

(A) Every living thing eventually grows old and dies. We refer to the life span of an animal as its longevity. In general, longevity is related to the size of the animal and how fast it grows. Animals in captivity often live longer than those in the wild. Sometimes, but not always, it may be that the animal faces harder living conditions in the wild. Mice, for example, live only a few months in the wild. Those same mice could survive two or three years in captivity.

(B) Among mammals, humans have the longest life span. Whales and elephants can live 60 years or more. But when you compare mammals to birds of the same size, the birds live longer.

(C) As a group, insects have the shortest life spans. At one extreme is the mayfly, which, once it is an adult, lives only a day or two at the most. At the other end are some beetles and termites. It has been speculated that a queen termite may live up to 50 years.

_____ 1. What creature lives only two days as an adult? _____

_____ 2. What is another way of saying life span? _____

_____ 3. Of same-sized mammals and birds, which live longer?_____

_____ 4. How long do mice live in the wild? _____

_____ 5. Queen termites may live up to 50 years. Fact or opinion? _____

_____ 6. Which mammal has the longest life span? _____

Give your opinion: If you were a mouse, would you rather live a short life in the wild or a longer one in captivity? Why? _____

_____

_____

Name: _____   **Date:** _____

Directions: As you read the story, think about what general statements could be made about the subject covered. Then answer the questions in two parts below.

The word "pencil" comes from a Latin word, penicillus, which means "little tail." When pencils were first invented centuries ago, they were not the kind of pencils we use today. The first pencils were actually small, fine-pointed brushes.

Although we call the substance in pencils "lead," it is largely made of a material called graphite and contains no actual lead. Graphite was first discovered about 500 years ago in a mine in Cumberland, England. Crude pencils similar to those we use today were first made from pure graphite.

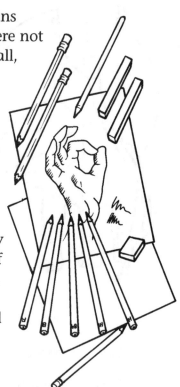

Later, in 1760, the Faber family of Germany pulverized graphite to make a kind of pencil, but their pencils did not prove to be successful. A useful pencil was not produced until later that century when, in 1795, Frenchman N. J. Conte pressed a ground mixture of graphite, water, and clay into sticks and fired them in a large oven called a kiln. The more clay that was added, the harder the "lead" would be. When more graphite was added, the pencil "lead" would be softer. Today, more than 350 different kinds of pencils are made with varying degrees of hardness, softness, intensity, and color. A standard Number 2 pencil has a lead softness level of 2 degrees.

Part A: True or false?

1. All pencils contain lead. _____

2. Pencils have remained pretty much the same since their invention. _____

3. The ratio of clay to graphite determines the hardness of a pencil. _____

4. Today a variety of pencils are made for different uses and effects. _____

Part B: Write one or two sentences that summarize the information given in the story.

_____

_____

Name: _____   **Date:** _____

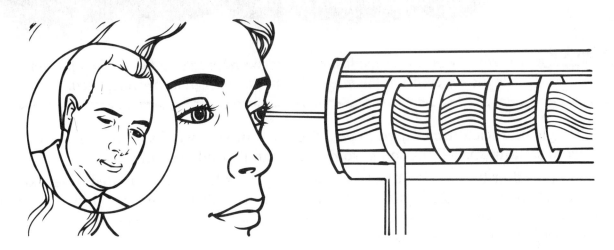

Lasers

A laser organizes irregular or jumbled light waves into a harmonious stream of light. The word "laser" is an acronym for Light Amplification by the Stimulated Emission of Radiation. In 1957, Theodore Maiman developed the idea of a laser based on the theories of light proposed by the great physicist, Albert Einstein. However, it was not until 1960 that Maiman built the first laser. This small but effective laser generated laser light by energizing a ruby crystal with light from a flash tube.

Since then, the development of lasers has continued to advance. We now use lasers for such varied things as performing surgery, scanning bar codes, cutting metal, reading information on compact discs, and carrying communication signals.

1. Lasers organize irregular and jumbled light into a harmonious stream.
   Lasers jumble harmonious streams of light into irregular patterns.

2. Though not all lasers are the same, they work essentially the same way.
   Different types of lasers work in different ways.

3. Only small lasers are effective.
   The first laser was small but effective.

4. Lasers are best used in surgery and for carrying communication signals.
   Lasers have a wide variety of practical uses.

If you've ever used a map to find your way, you know that a map is just a visual way to show information. Let's try it.

Directions: *The story below traces the history of crossword puzzles. After reading it carefully, write the key events in the map below in the order that they happened.*

Some people in ancient times used to pass the time making word squares. The letters in these word squares spelled the same words horizontally and vertically.

In 1913, the editor for the *New York World* newspaper, Arthur Winn, created a new kind of word square. Winn called his puzzle a "word cross." This first crossword puzzle appeared in the Sunday edition of the paper on December 21 of that year. The readers of the paper enjoyed it so much that they asked for more.

However, it wasn't until 1924 that the first book of crossword puzzles was published. The book started an overnight craze. People competed in national tournaments, and some libraries had to enforce a five-minute limit for dictionary use. While crossword enthusiasts may not be as fanatical today, the crossword puzzle is still a popular pastime.

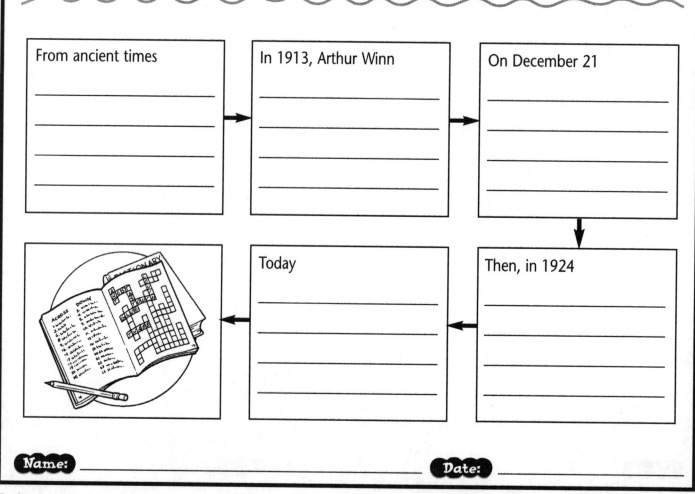

From ancient times

_____
_____
_____
_____

In 1913, Arthur Winn

_____
_____
_____
_____

On December 21

_____
_____
_____
_____

Today

_____
_____
_____
_____

Then, in 1924

_____
_____
_____
_____

Name: _____   **Date:** _____

'Round the World

On September 20, 1519, a fleet of five vessels was outfitted and ready to leave Spain. Their commander, Ferdinand Magellan, was familiar with the waters of the Atlantic as far south as the equator. The plan was to find a passage through the continent of South America. For months he searched along the east coast without success.

In August, Magellan sent out two ships to scout a wide inlet. Upon their return they reported seeing a large bay beyond. Magellan navigated through the straight, which was perilous. Undaunted, he pressed on. After 38 grueling days, Magellan reached a great ocean. He named it the Pacific because it looked so peaceful.

Although Magellan greatly underestimated the size of the Pacific, he continued sailing westward. Supplies ran out and many of the crew perished. Still, Magellan made it as far as the Philippines, where he died in a battle on April 27, 1521.

Magellan is given credit for being the first person to circumnavigate the world because, though he didn't complete the voyage, he did reach a point further west than he had previously reached sailing east.

Almost three years to the day after the fleet set sail, one lone ship, Victoria, made it back to Spain where they had originally set out.

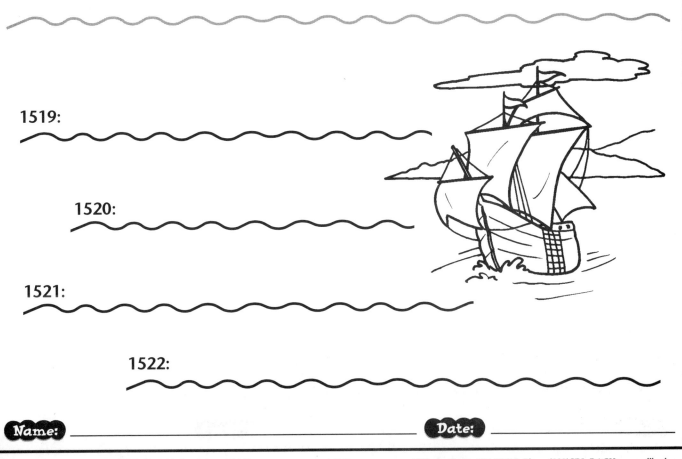

1519:

1520:

1521:

1522:

Name: _____   Date: _____

Mark Twain was quite a character. Read about him below. Then complete the character map about him.

Man of Many Faces

You could probably identify a picture of this man as Mark Twain, famous author of such classic tales as *Tom Sawyer* and *The Adventures of Huckleberry Finn*.

Mark Twain was a man of many faces. He was a newspaper man, a steamboat pilot, and even tried his hand at gold mining. But, he found his true calling in observing people and writing about them.

What you may not realize is that Mark Twain is a pseudonym—a name Samuel Clemens used for his writing. Where did he come up with this name? It just so happens that in his day (mid 1800s) riverboat pilots used the term "mark twain" to mean the water was 2 fathoms, or 12 feet, deep.

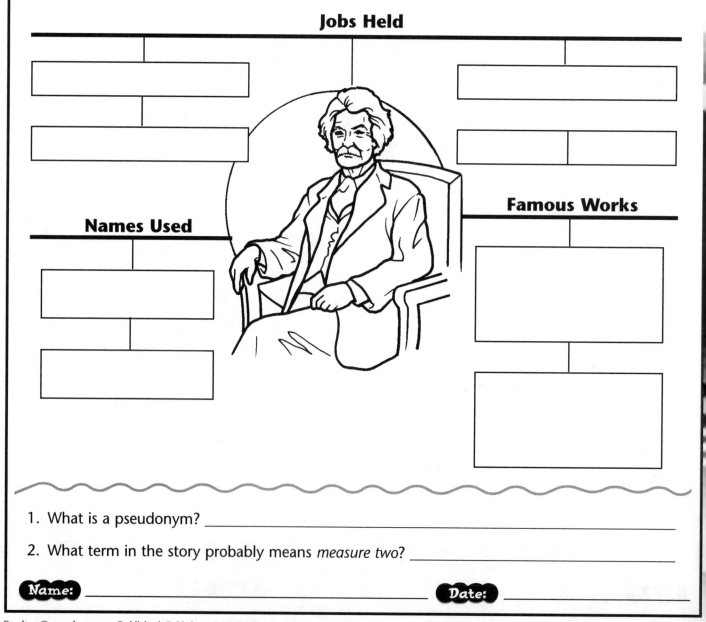

Jobs Held

Names Used

Famous Works

1. What is a pseudonym? _____

2. What term in the story probably means *measure two*? _____

Visualization is an important tool that you can use to map out a story in your mind. Below, the events in a story about Amy are out of order. First, number the sentences in sequence. Next, illustrate what you visualized. Finally, write what you think might happen next based on your mental map of the story.

The New Team

_____ Mom called the number on the flyer to get more information.

_____ The flyer was inviting boys and girls her age to join the team.

_____ On sign-up day, Amy and her mom went to the community park.

_____ Each person was to try to kick the ball into the net.

_____ Amy saw a flyer announcing the formation of a new youth soccer team.

_____ The coach introduced himself and explained the program.

_____ Amy showed it to her mom and asked if she could join.

_____ Then he asked the children to form a line on the field.

When Amy's turn came, the coach handed her the ball and...

_____

_____

_____

Name: _____ **Date:** _____

1. Ned just got his driver's license.
2. Phil is about to retire after 40 years in the insurance industry.
3. Lynn is married and has two children under the age of ten.
4. Dave just got a degree in accounting and is starting his first full-time job.
5. Ken just learned to tie his own shoes.
6. Tom is attending his grandson's wedding next month.
7. Rose is starting first grade this year.
8. Betty has a daughter who just graduated from college.
9. Josh earns money by mowing lawns and having a paper route.
10. Jim just had his 20th anniversary with the same company.

Name: _____   **Date:** _____

Scope & Sequence

Students	root words/word origins	prefixes/suffixes	following directions	visual/context clues	vocabulary	signal words	dictionary	idioms/similies/metaphors	five W's	classification	analogies	compare/contrast	questioning techniques	prediction	inferences	main idea	outlining	summarize	problem/solution	graphic devices

Scope & Sequence

Students	fact/opinion/exaggeration	fact/fantasy	trivial/redundant information	story genre	topic/supporting sentences	compare/contrast-fact/opinion	cause/effect	character analysis	perspective analysis	inferences	factual recall	author's view/purpose	character's view/purpose	setting analysis	time analysis	read to inform/persuade	story sequence	generalizations	story mapping	character mapping

Answer Key

Page 6
century, J
manufacture, H
democracy, C
fortify, D
terrarium, G
relocate, F
aquatics, K
telegram, E
autograph, B
predict, A
incredible, I
liberty, l

Page 7
1. a
2. c
3. b
4. a
5. b
6. a
7. a
8. b
9. c
10. a
11. a

Page 8
Disappear, rewrite, misunderstood, multicolor, midday, nonsense, unnecessary, international
1. multicolored
2. disappear
3. unnecessary
4. misunderstood
5. rewrite
6. midday
7. international
8. nonsense

Page 9
1. underfur
2. indisputable
3. incessant
4. retreated
5. intrusion
6. subspecies
7. undaunted
8. interbreed
9. untamed

Page 10
1. confidently
2. dejectedly
3. wearily
4. jubilantly
5. nervously
6. suspiciously

Page 11
1. accumulation
2. translation
3. promotion
4. formation
5. mention
6. prevention
7. station
8. description
9. population
10. punctuation

Page 12
1. Begin with a sheet of rectangular…
2. Once you have cut off the strip…
3. Fold (A) down…
4. Fold up corners (B) and (C)…
5. Color…

Page 13
1. g
2. a
3. b
4. h
5. f
6. d
7. c
8. e
imminent

Page 14
1. evolution
2. east
3. mammals
4. one of a kind
5. refuge
6. 20%
7. it is an island

Page 15
Dr. Windom/archaeologist
Mrs. Tandy/tailor, seamstress
Capt. Jones/pilot
Ms. Lopez/scientist
Mr. Synder/sports coach
Dr. Huang/dentist
Mrs. Tyler/lawyer
Capt. Allen/police captain

Page 16
1. True
2. False
3. Doesn't say
4. True
5. Doesn't say
6. True
7. True
8. False
9. True

Page 17
1 boy
2. James Connor
3. cousins
4. Sara White
5. Lynn Connor
6. Chris Connor
7. Beth Connor
8. Jim Connor
9. 3
10. yes
11. Neil King
12. Neil King and Jean Connor

Page 18
1. truck
2. disrespectful
3. followed
4. all-natural
5. farm; rural
6. collected
7. overhead covering
8. honest; open
9. visible
10. tale; story

Page 19
1. elated
2. disappointed
3. foolish
4. insulted
5. remorseful

Page 20
1. remembering
2. sticking out
3. shelter
4. feeding livestock
5. well-known
6. pull it up
7. reasonable
8. fake
9. a large number
10. troubled and annoyed

Page 21
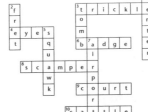

Page 22
Part 1:
1. however
2. immediately
3. probably
4. toward
5. such as
Part 2:
1. alongside
2. consequently
3. always
4. in spite of
5. due to

Page 23
1. signals more to come
2. signals a comparison
3. signals a conclusion
4. signals more to come
5. shows sequence
6. signals an example
7. signals a direction change
8. signals an important point
9. signals a conclusion
10. signals importance
11. shows uncertainty

Page 24
A. 4
B. 10
C. 7
D. 5
E. 8
F. 9
G. 1
H. 6
I. 2
J. 3
K. 6
L. 5
M. 5
N. 4

Page 25
1. fruit pies
2. cottage cheese
3. money
4. wool
5. head
6. metal rod
7. grain

Page 26
1. 180
2. 179
3. 181
4. other

5. 179
6. 182
7. 180
8. 181
9. 178
10. 182
11. 180
12. other
13. 179
14. 178

Page 27
(Wording of meanings will vary.)
• aesthetics
• prestige
• focal
• myriad
• integral

Page 28
1. present from Grandma
2. his Uncle Jack
3. laundry
4. noodles
5. his pet rabbit
6. a suit
7. a photo album
8. four grandparents

Page 29
1. pouch
2. claws
3. nose
4. tail
5. bean
6. back
7. possums
8. possum

Page 30
(Answers will vary)
suggested:
1. a sudden realization
2. in trouble
3. respect my privacy
4. by a narrow margin
5. write a note/letter
6. quickly/accurately
7. seems to go by swiftly
8. spend time with
9. got my attention
10. agree on things

Page 31
1. metaphor
2. metaphor
3. neither
4. simile
5. simile
6. simile
7. neither

8. simile
9. metaphor

Page 32
1. butterflies
2. tree bark
3. to blend in with their environment
4. when they are at rest
5. cocoons
6. They both have antenna.

Page 33
1. in the 1950s
2. a surfer
3. young people
4. in pedestrian traffic areas
5. 55 MPH

Page 34

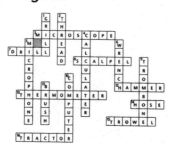

Page 35
(Accept any logical conclusion.)
1. towels; the rest are used for washing
2. nests; the only one not enclosed
3. yogurt; the only one not a liquid
4. lamp; the only one not wooden
5. soup; the rest are sandwich fixings
6. screwdriver, the only item not a garden tool

Page 36
1. strings
2. actor
3. fly
4. man
5. taste
6. holiday
7. planet
8. flower
9. puppy
10. mice
11. garage
12. water

13. tree
14. bakery
15. dirt

Page 37
1. chili
2. twelve
3. success
4. eat
5. bright
6. him
7. slept
8. sheep
9. vegetable
10. books
11. Chinese
12. minister
13. herb
14. scarlet
15. grimace
16. remote
17. lean
18. pavement

Page 38
1. Fact
2. Opinion
3. Fact
4. Opinion
5. Opinion
6. Fact
7. Fact
8. Opinion

Page 39
Math: interest rate, multiplication, percentage
Science: endangered species, parallel circuit, transpiration, static electricity, carnivore
Measurement: centimeter, right angle
Social Studies: unconstitutional, legislature, Civil War, veto
Geography: hemisphere, compass rose, Europe, territory, cartographer, isthmus

Page 40
Diet: insects, fruit, pollen, reptiles, fish, small animals
Body Parts: sharp claws, sharp teeth, wings
Characteristics: flying mammal, astute hearing

Page 41
1. True
2. False
3. Doesn't say (but could be inferred as true)
4. True
5. Doesn't say (but could be inferred as true)
6. True
7. False
8. Doesn't say

Page 42
A, B, A, B, A, B, A, B, B, A

Page 43
1. B
2. B
3. D
4. P
5. B
6. D
7. D
8. P

Page 44
(Questions will vary but must refer to missing information.)
1. Who do I contact?
2. What is its age and condition?
3. What is for sale?
4. How much do they cost?
5. What size are they?
6. What is the age or condition?

Page 45
1. sausage, hotdogs (or frankfurters)
2. detail
3. Answers will vary.
4. Paragraph 1
5. Answers will vary.
6. Answers will vary.

Page 46
1. a cellular phone
2. popcorn
3. a cat
4. pudding
5. a tooth
6. hair
7. a turtle
8. a comb
9. a carrot

Page 47
1 we took him to the vet.
2. she had to pay a fine.

3. we took the bus to the mall.
4. he uses a cane.
5. we went to the bank.
6. school was closed today.
7. we went to the pet store.
8. she went to the library.

Page 48
1. on a ship
2. in a graveyard
3. at a shoe store
4. in a tent
5. in a library

Page 49
1. Antarctica
2. Nile
3. Japan
4. Mediterranean sea
5. Australia

Page 50
1. farmer
2. police officer
3. bank teller
4. science teacher
5. computer technician
6. book salesperson
7. dog trainer

Page 51
1. no penguins live in Alaska.
2. she is taking care of her teeth.
3. Dan will not eat meat.
4. he has more females than males.
5. it is likely to rain tomorrow.
6. Janet is the middle child.
7. Main is south of Rick's and Cole's.
8. All other stars are farther away.

Page 52
1. pickup truck
2. refrigerator
3. set of encyclopedias
4. computer
5. kittens
6. baby items
7. set of silverware

Page 53
• They have eyes, appendages...

• But some have six, four,...
• The fangs are used to...
• Some use them to crush...

Page 54
1. 106-110
2. Chapter 7, Sect. III
3. What is Pollution/ Chief Sources of Pollution
4. 93-94
5. Chapter 7, Sect. II
6. Chapter 8, Sect. III
7. no; yes

Page 55
Answers will vary.

Page 56
(Sentences checked)
The girl knows how to read.
The scene takes place in the past.
The house has a fireplace.

Page 57
1. M
2. V
3. B
4. V
5. B
6. M
7. M
8. V

Page 58
(A)
1. D
2. D
3. MI
(B)
1. MI
2. D
3. D
(C)
1. D
2. D
3. MI
(D)
1. D
2. MI
3. D

Page 59
1. False
2. Doesn't say
3. True

4. False
5. Doesn't say
6. Doesn't say
7. False
8. Doesn't say

Page 60
(Suggest order)
The group of spiders known as orb...
These spiders generally have bodies that...
Orb spiders depend entirely on...
They usually construct a web...
When finished with the web...

Page 61
1. Newbery medal
2. Frederic G. Melcher
3. once a year
4. 1997
5. magazines
6. American Library Association
7. England
8. artist

Page 62
1. Hares and rabbits have distinct differences.
2. Don't Call Me a Rabbit
3. Like rabbits, hares come in a wide variety...
4. Hares are often mistakenly called rabbits.

Page 63
1. nothing
2. No. Shooting stars are Meteors.
3. Meteorite
4. The glowing heat caused by friction in the atmosphere.
5. Answers will vary.
6. Meteors

Page 64
1. An X ray is a special way to take a picture of a bone, tooth, or object concealed from direct sight.
2. Crossed out: (A) At the dentist...
(B) The X ray process was discovered...

3. Answers will vary.
4. Answers will vary.
5. Answers will vary.

Page 65
(Answers/wording may vary.)
1. to define and explain acronyms
2. A palindrome is a word spelled...
3. It is an acronym and gives information about acronyms.
4. FYI, ASAP, BLT, ZIP, IQ, PC (and/or others)
5. Yes. It fits the definition given.
6. They are short or single words, not a series of words.

Page 67
I South America is the fourth...
A. The land is...
B. Most of the population...
II The continent of South America...
A. Its chief agricultural exports are...
B. Minerals such as...
III One of South America's outstanding...
A. Covering an area...
IV South America's vast...
A. The largest numbers...
B. Many people...

Page 68
1. One type of beetle can sense the presence of fire.
2. The Amazing Melanophia.
Summaries will vary.

Page 69
Summaries will vary.

Page 70
1. Yes
2. No
3. No
4. Yes
5. Yes
6. Yes
7. Yes

8. Yes
9. Yes

Page 71
1. Abby
2. September
3. Abby's dog
4. Collingsville
5. Abby's grandparents
6. Abby to visit
7. Liz misses Abby
8. Answers will vary.

Page 72
1. Unknown
2. Yes
3. No
4. Yes
5. Yes
6. No
7. Unknown
8. Yes
9. Unknown
10. Yes
11. Yes
12. No

Page 73
1. through the leaves
2. through the roots
3. It produces its own food.

Page 74
1. 70
2. 180
3. 72%
4. 35
5. 48
6. less
7. low
8. 350
9. 12
10. 5
11. saturated fat 20

Page 75
Answers will vary.

Page 76

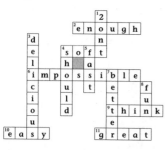

Page 77
1. F
2. T
3. T
4. T
5. T
6. F
7. F
8. T

Page 78
(checked)
The Harlem Globetrotters have played…
The Globetrotter team was founded…
Their theme song is…
The Globetrotters scored 8,829…
It took a team of retired NBA players…
The players were known for their…
The Globetrotters have also been…

Page 79
(A)
1. underlined: The word sphinx refers to an imaginary…
2. crossed out: The pyramids are very old.
3. False
(B)
1. underlined: Death Valley seems like a harsh name…
2. crossed out: Not many people live there.
3. name

Page 80
(A)
1. underlined: Molting is the name of…
2. crossed out: It is really weird to…
3. Answers will vary.
(B)
1. underlined: But mint is actually…
2. crossed out: Peppermint is a…
3. Answers will vary.

Page 81
(A) I 3; The paragraph describes parakeets , not

where to buy one.
II a. true, Sentence 1
b. true, Sentence 4
c. false, Sentence 2
(B) I 5; The paragraph is about the flounder, not all animals that use camouflage.
II a. false, Sentence 2
b. true Sentence 3
c. true, Sentence 4

Page 82
1. newspaper
2. thesaurus
3. schedule
4. letter
5. dictionary
6. novel
7. manual
8. recipe

Page 83
(Reasons will vary.)
1. fantasy
2. realistic fiction
3. historical fiction
4. biography

Page 84
1. Silk cloth has been…
2. silk thread is made by worms
3. silkworms
4. millennium
5. yes
6. mulberry leaves
7. natural

Page 85
1. She said she was having lots of fun, but the best…
2. New Mexico
3. hot-air
4. just after sunrise
5. ascent, descent
6. answers may vary.

Page 86
(A)
1. D
2. MI
3. D
(B)
1. MI
2. D
3. D
(C)
1. D
2. D
3. MI

(D)
1. D
2. MI
3. D

Page 87
Crossed out: Butterflies are prettier than moths.
Can you tell butterflies and moths…
Both are insects…
Butterflies rest their wings…
Butterflies have slender…
It should be easy to tell…

Page 88
(A)
1. D
2. MI
3. D
(B)
1. MI
2. D
3. D
(C)
1. D
2. MI
3. D
(D)
1. D
2. D
3. MI

Page 89
Labeled: clam, chiton, conch, tusk
1. Seashells come in a wide variety. People admire…
2. Four basic kinds… Univalves…
3. They were created by mollusks.
4. external
5. kind

Page 90
Answers will vary.

Page 91
1. both
2. orange
3. neither
4. orange
5. both
6. apple
7. apple
8. apple

Page 92
Alike: bats, mammals, front and back legs

<u>Different:</u> squirrel can only glide
Squirrel has furry flaps instead of wings.

Page 93
1. True
2. False
3. False
4. False
5. False
6. True
7. True
8. False
9. False

Page 94
1. Fact
2. Doesn't say
3. Opinion
4. Fact
5. Fact
6. Fact
7. Fact*
8. Fact*
9. Fact*
*May be considered opinions because the story infers the information but does not give it as direct fact.

Page 95
Answers will vary.

Page 96
1. rode his bike through some puddles.
2. overslept this morning.
3. forgot my lunch money.
4. didn't have a map.
5. was making noise in the library.
6. was sold out.
7. needed the number for Pizza King.
8. moved last month.

Page 97
1. affect
2. effect
3. effect
4. effect
5. affect
6. effect
7. effect
8. affect
9. affect
10. effect
11. affect
12. affect
13. effect
14. affect
15. affect
16. effect
17. effect
18. affect

Page 98
1. the horse/Lisa's dad
2. understanding; supportive
3. She was mad.
4. woman
5. No/reasons will vary.
6. Answers will vary.

Page 99
1. thoughtful
2. The letter went to her granddaughter.
3. They allowed him to write the letter to Ellie Rivers.
4. He wrote the letter.
5. He was trying to solve a mystery and find a particular person.
6. Answers will vary.

Page 100
1. Story does not say.
2. We don't know.
3. An unknown human narrator.
4. Modern medicine.
5. Answers will vary.

Page 101
1. from someone who lives in L.A.
2. The author likes L.A. He/she thinks the airport is great.
3. Answers will vary.
4. Answers will vary.

Page 102
1. True
2. Can't be determined
3. Can't be determined
4. True
5. Can't be determined
6. False

Page 103
1. All use electricity in some form.
2. to kill prey or defend itself

3. Yes/The story says it has predators.
4. surprising; electrical stimulation
5. strong; good sized
6. Answers will vary.

Page 104
1. castle
2. a pelican
3. a star
4. a bike
5. an army
6. a roast
7. the phone
8. a jacket
9. his little sister

Page 105
1. 2, 1, 3
2. 3, 2, 1
3. 1, 2, 3
4. 2, 3, 1
5. 2, 1, 3
6. 2, 3, 1
7. 3, 1, 2
8. 3, 1, 2

Page 106
1. what each individual boy's time was
2. how long each stop was
3. what size battery her toy takes
4. how many total attended the picnic

Page 107
1. True
2. Doesn't say
3. False
4. Doesn't say
5. True

Page 108
1. G
2. NG
3. G
4. G
5. G
6. NG
7. NG
8. G
9. NG

Page 109
1. 24
2. breastbone
3. False
4. spine

5. false ribs
6. invertebrate
7. the upper 3 sets of false ribs

Page 110
1. swaggering
2. the sunshine
3. mixture
4. true
5. The weather in southern California...

Page 111
1. Japan
2. The author enjoys growing bonsai trees.
3. Bonsai trees are considered a symbol of immortality. Bonsai is the Japanese art of producing miniature, fully formed trees.
4. harmony, balance, beauty, and simplicity
5. Answers will vary.

Page 112
1. a cute neighborhood cat
2. a nice lady who doesn't bother him
3. It was secluded and comfortable.
4. She remained still so she would not be noticed.
5. She was worried Gus would attack the dove's nest.

Page 113
1. man: frustrated, angry; donkey: stubborn, hungry
2. man: to sell his wares; donkey: vegetables
3. man: I'll never make money; donkey: I'm not moving.
4. Man: Get moving!; donkey: I'm tired!
Answers will vary.

Page 114
1. future
2. present
3. past
4. past

Page 115

1 camping in the woods
2. in King Arthur's Court
3. in the outback of Australia
4. the top of Mt. Everest
5. in the heart of Africa

Page 116
1. 1610 A.D.; crude telescope
2. prehistoric; wooly mammoth
3. 1999 A.D.; space
4. 1492 A.D.; ship, Native American, European

Page 117
Sun: made a card
Mon: got an A on the test
Tues: got invited to a party; made a cake
Wed: Mom's birthday; Dad cooked
Thurs:
Fri: math quiz; went to the mall
Sat: Jenny's party

Page 118
Answers will vary.

Page 119
1. A girl gets a birthday surprise.
2. It was her birthday.
3. in the evening
4. her feelings
5. middle child
6. disappointed

Page 120
Answers will vary.

Page 121
1. same
2. different
3. happy
4. new, silly, sweet, barefoot
5. sad
6. heavy, sagging, drooping, thirsty
7. summer

Page 122
1. False
2. False
3. True
4. False
5. True

6. False
7. True
The Celts were a network of tribes…

Page 123
1. Tina Meller being absent for…
2. Imperfect Timing
3. to entertain the reader
4. a surprise turn in a direction…
5. Answers will vary.

Page 124
1. Yes
2. No
3. No
4. Yes
5. No
6. No
7. Yes
8. No

Page 125
Answers will vary.

Page 126
• Their pictures were on the walls…
• He asked Dad if they could…
• Sure enough, he got to see…
• "How did they know…?" he asked.

Page 127
Underlined: when it comes to building things…
Crossed out: Uncle Cal is my
Order:
When it comes to building things…
Once, Uncle Cal built a shed…
Then he made a super doghouse…
Plus, when Grandma wanted…
And, he does all this on weekends…

Page 128
1. at an airport
2. Josh was going to visit his dad.
3. traveling alone
4. He had mixed feelings.

5. to show he was brave
6. for the weekend
7. Answers will vary, or to make him feel at ease

Page 129
1. C; the Mayfly
2. A; how long something lives
3. B; birds live longer
4. A; a few months
5. C; Fact
6. B; humans

Page 130
(A)
1. false
2. false
3. true
4. true
(B)
Answers will vary.

Page 131
1. Lasers organize irregular…
2. Different types of lasers…
3. The first laser was small…
4. Lasers have a wide variety…

Page 132
Ancient times: people passed time making word squares
Arthur Winn: created new kind of word square
Dec. 21: first crossword puzzle appeared in the paper
1924: first book of crosswords published
Today: crossword puzzles very popular

Page 133
1519: fleet from Spain set out…
1520: Magellan named the Pacific Ocean.
1521: Magellan died in battle.
1522: Victoria made it back to Spain.

Page 134
Jobs held: author newspaperman

steamboat pilot
gold miner
Names: Mark Twain
Samuel Clemens
Famous Works: *Tom Sawyer, The Adventures of Huckleberry Finn*
1. another name
2. Mark Twain

Page 135
Order: 4, 2, 5, 7, 1, 6, 3, 8
Illustrations and answers will vary.

Page 136
Order: Ken, Rose, Josh, Ned, Dave, Lynn
Order: Jim, Betty, Phil, Tom